Title Page

Revenue, Growth, and Development for Muslim Communities

By

Fazal Abubakkar Esaf

Copyright Page

First Edition: 2026

The strategies, frameworks, and models presented in this book are intended solely for educational, developmental, and informational purposes. The author and publisher disclaim any responsibility for outcomes resulting from business, financial, or investment decisions made based on the contents of this book.

Table of Contents

"Wealth is not the accumulation of gold, but the empowerment of people, the cultivation of knowledge, and the dignity of community."

— **Fazal Abubakkar Esaf**

Dedication

To the visionaries and community builders who refuse to accept limitation,

and to every citizen who believes that prosperity is a right—not a privilege.

Acknowledgments

No transformative vision is realized in isolation.

I extend my sincere gratitude to the community leaders, economists, and urban planners who contributed insights on sustainable development and inclusive growth. I am equally thankful to the researchers, strategists, and entrepreneurs who continue to translate theory into real-world impact.

To my mentors, family, and peers—your unwavering encouragement, honest critique, and grounded perspective have been invaluable. This work stands on the foundation of your guidance and belief.

Preface

Prosperity is not accidental, nor is it inherited—it is intentionally designed, strategically planned, and consistently executed.

This book is written for nations, states, cities, and neighborhoods seeking to transform their resources into sustainable, ethical, and inclusive wealth. It offers a comprehensive 360-degree blueprint—from macroeconomic policy frameworks to neighborhood-level initiatives—for generating revenue, building resilience, and strengthening social prosperity.

Through a combination of strategic models, actionable checklists, policy frameworks, and business canvas approaches, readers will learn how to:

- Identify and unlock latent resources
- Align institutional, community, and economic goals
- Implement both innovative and traditional revenue streams
- Measure progress with transparency, accountability, and data-driven metrics

Whether you are a policymaker, entrepreneur, institutional leader, or community organizer, this book provides a practical and actionable roadmap toward economic independence and sustainable growth.

Introduction

Muslim communities—like all societies—possess vast, untapped economic and human potential. However, structural challenges such as fragmented governance, underutilized assets, and shifting global economic pressures often limit progress.

This book addresses these challenges through a structured, multi-level approach:

- **National-Level Strategies:** Trade policy, energy development, innovation ecosystems, and taxation frameworks
- **State-Level Strategies:** Industrial clusters, education systems, healthcare infrastructure, and public–private partnerships
- **City-Level Strategies:** Urban planning, smart infrastructure, creative economies, and municipal revenue systems
- **Neighborhood-Level Strategies:** Micro-entrepreneurship, cultural enterprises, local skills development, and cooperative models

By integrating policy, business, technology, and cultural values, this work presents a holistic 360-degree framework for building thriving, resilient, and prosperous communities.

Epigraph

"Wealth is not the accumulation of gold, but the empowerment of people, the cultivation of knowledge, and the dignity of community."

— **Fazal Abubakkar Esaf**

Chapter 1 — Understanding Economic Sovereignty

Objective

Economic sovereignty is the cornerstone of any prosperous community, city, or nation. It extends beyond political independence to encompass the capacity to generate, manage, and deploy resources without excessive reliance on external forces.

This chapter equips communities, states, and neighborhoods to:

- Define self-sufficiency and fiscal independence
- Understand strategic planning frameworks for sustainable growth
- Map resources, identify revenue gaps, and diversify income streams
- Implement practical tools, policies, and measurable metrics for long-term economic autonomy

Why Economic Sovereignty Matters

Economic sovereignty ensures long-term resilience, empowerment, sustainability, and strategic growth.

A sovereign economy enables communities to withstand global shocks such as recessions, commodity price fluctuations, and supply disruptions. It empowers citizens and local leadership with decision-making autonomy and reduces dependence on foreign aid, debt, or volatile external income sources.

Most importantly, sovereignty enables controlled reinvestment into infrastructure, education, healthcare, and innovation—ensuring prosperity for future generations.

Economic sovereignty does **not** mean isolation. It represents **strategic autonomy**—the ability to engage globally while maintaining fiscal independence and internal stability.

Case Studies: Learning From Proven Models

Several regions have successfully transitioned toward economic sovereignty through diversification, strategic governance, and leveraging cultural assets.

Malaysia

Diversified from oil dependence into halal manufacturing, Islamic finance, and tourism. Its halal economy evolved into a major global export sector.

Dubai, UAE

Transformed from an oil-based economy into a global hub for tourism, real estate, aviation, and finance through infrastructure development and regulatory reform.

Istanbul, Turkey

Leveraged its cultural heritage and geographic positioning to build strong tourism, education, and entrepreneurial ecosystems.

Key Takeaways

- Economic diversification is essential
- Cultural and religious assets can be monetized ethically
- Strong governance and strategic planning accelerate growth

Plan: Mapping Resources and Identifying Gaps

1. Resource Inventory

Resource Category	**Key Components**
Natural Resources	Land, water, minerals, renewable energy
Human Capital	Workforce skills, labor availability, education levels
Financial Assets	Government budgets, savings, local investments
Cultural Capital	Heritage sites, religious tourism, arts, crafts

2. Revenue Analysis

Area	Key Actions
Current Income Mapping	Taxes, fees, grants, business revenue
External Dependence	Measure reliance on aid, loans, remittances
Revenue Gaps	Identify unstable income sources and unused assets

3. Stakeholder Assessment

Stakeholder Group	Role in Economic Flow
Government	Policy, taxation, infrastructure
Community Leaders	Social mobilization and governance
Business Owners	Job creation and local investment
Religious Institutions	Social finance, waqf, charity systems

Strategy: Diversifying Revenue Streams

1. Taxation

Strategy	Action
Progressive Tax Systems	Fair property, income, and business taxation
Formalization	Encourage informal businesses to register
Compliance	Simplify processes to increase tax participation

2. Trade and Exports

Sector	Opportunity
Halal Industry	Food, pharmaceuticals, cosmetics
Textiles	Local production and export branding
Technology	Software, digital services, outsourcing

3. Services and Tourism

Segment	Development Focus
Religious Tourism	Pilgrimage circuits, heritage tours
Education Services	Universities, vocational institutes
Healthcare	Medical tourism and specialized clinics

4. Investments and Sovereign Funds

Investment Area	Objective
Sovereign/Community Funds	Long-term asset building
Energy & Infrastructure	Stable and recurring returns
Startups & Tech Parks	Innovation-driven growth

Risk Assessment and Mitigation

Risk	Impact	Mitigation Strategy
Economic Shocks	High	Diversified revenue and emergency funds
Political Instability	Medium	Transparent governance and participatory councils
Single-Sector Dependence	High	Multi-sector growth strategies
Resource Depletion	Medium	Renewable energy and sustainability programs

Tools and Techniques

Tool	Purpose
SWOT Analysis	Identify strengths, weaknesses, opportunities, threats
PESTEL Analysis	Assess macro-environment factors
GIS Mapping	Track geographic and resource distribution
Fiscal Modeling Software	Predict revenue and simulate policy outcomes

Community Engagement Tactics

Method	Purpose
Participatory Budgeting	Citizens decide funding priorities
Public Forums & Workshops	Transparency and policy dialogue
Crowdsourcing Ideas	Community-driven revenue initiatives

Economic Sovereignty Metrics

Metric	Description
Revenue Independence Ratio	% of locally generated income
Diversification Index	Number of stable revenue streams
Citizen Participation Rate	% engaged in local economy
Local GDP Contribution	Share from domestic industries

Policy Recommendations

Policy Area	Recommendation
SME Development	Incentivize small and medium enterprises
Tax Reform	Improve fairness, transparency, and efficiency
Strategic Sectors	Invest in agriculture, technology, halal industries
Partnerships	Expand public–private partnerships (PPP)

Step-by-Step Implementation Guide

Timeline	Action	Expected Outcome
Year 1	Resource audit and revenue gap analysis	Baseline economic understanding
Year 2	Pilot new revenue streams	Feasibility validation
Years 3–5	Scale successful models	Increased local revenue
Years 5–10	Full system integration	Self-sustaining economy

Blueprint: 10-Year Fiscal Roadmap

1. Establish a **Community Economic Council** composed of experts and stakeholders
2. Conduct a comprehensive audit of all natural, financial, and cultural assets
3. Develop a revenue gap analysis to prioritize sectors
4. Set annual targets for taxation, trade, services, and investments
5. Implement real-time monitoring and reporting systems
6. Launch pilot projects in high-priority sectors

7. Review progress annually and refine strategies
8. Reallocate resources based on performance data
9. Engage citizens continuously for accountability and transparency

Business Canvas: Economic Sovereignty Model

Block	**Details**
Value Proposition	Self-sustaining and resilient communities
Key Activities	Resource audits, planning, revenue optimization
Key Resources	Human capital, financial assets, natural/cultural resources
Key Partners	Businesses, NGOs, religious institutions, universities
Revenue Streams	Taxes, trade, services, investment returns
Customer Segments	Citizens, entrepreneurs, investors
Channels	Policy reforms, digital platforms, public engagement
Customer Relationships	Transparent, participatory, trust-based
Cost Structure	Council operations, audits, infrastructure investments
Metrics	Diversification index, fiscal independence ratio, participation rate

Conclusion

Economic sovereignty is both a mindset and a strategic system.

By systematically mapping resources, diversifying income streams, engaging citizens, and implementing structured economic planning, communities and nations can:

- Withstand external economic shocks

- Empower citizens and institutions
- Build sustainable social, cultural, and economic prosperity

Economic sovereignty is not a distant vision—it is a structured, achievable pathway toward dignity, stability, and long-term growth.

Chapter 2 — Mapping Resources and Capabilities

Objective

Before any community, city, or nation can pursue economic sovereignty, it must first develop a complete and accurate understanding of its resources and capabilities.

This chapter presents a structured and practical framework to map assets, evaluate economic potential, and identify critical gaps—forming the foundation for sustainable prosperity and strategic development.

Why Resource Mapping is Critical

Resource mapping is the first step toward effective economic planning and strategic decision-making.

It enables:

- **Informed Decision-Making** — Understanding available assets allows targeted investment
- **Efficient Allocation** — Resources are deployed where they deliver maximum impact
- **Identification of Untapped Potential** — Hidden opportunities in human, cultural, and natural capital emerge
- **Risk Reduction** — Early detection of dependencies and vulnerabilities

Without a clear understanding of resources, economic planning becomes speculative. With it, growth becomes measurable, strategic, and scalable.

Step 1 — Categorize Resources

A comprehensive resource inventory must include all major forms of capital:

Resource Categories

Resource Type	Key Components
Natural Resources	Land (arable, urban, industrial), water systems, minerals, renewable energy
Human Capital	Education levels, skills, workforce demographics, entrepreneurship potential, leadership capacity
Financial Resources	Public and private funds, investment flows, savings rates, tax base
Cultural & Social Capital	Heritage sites, religious institutions, festivals, crafts, community networks
Technological & Infrastructure Assets	ICT infrastructure, internet access, transport systems, utilities, research institutions

Step 2 — Assess Resource Capacity and Potential

Once resources are identified, they must be evaluated in terms of productivity, value, and sustainability.

Assessment Methods

- **Resource Audit** — Quantitative and qualitative evaluation
- **Capacity Mapping** — Determine which resources can generate revenue, social value, or infrastructure support
- **Risk Identification** — Detect dependencies such as single-sector reliance or external funding

Checklist — Resource Assessment

Resource Type	Inventory Complete	Potential Utilization	Risks Identified
Natural			
Human			
Financial			
Cultural			
Technological			

Step 3 — Identify Gaps and Opportunities

After assessment, compare **current utilization vs. maximum potential.**

Key Focus Areas

- Identify **critical gaps** such as skill shortages, underused land, or weak infrastructure
- Detect **high-value opportunities** such as:
  - Exportable halal products
  - Renewable energy zones
  - Creative and cultural industry hubs

Blueprint Example — Resource Gap Analysis

Resource	Current Status	Potential Use	Revenue Opportunity	Risk Level
Land	30% urbanized	Agri-tech parks	$5M/year	Medium
Workforce	60% skilled	Tech start-ups	$3M/year	Low
Cultural Assets	10 heritage sites	Tourism & festivals	$2M/year	Low

Step 4 — Stakeholder Mapping

Economic development requires coordinated action among all stakeholders influencing resource flow.

Key Actors

- Government departments (finance, trade, culture, education)
- Local businesses and investors
- NGOs and community organizations
- Religious institutions and community leadership

Checklist — Stakeholder Engagement

Requirement	Status
Stakeholder registry completed	
Contact persons identified	
Engagement methods defined (forums, surveys, workshops)	
Roles and responsibilities assigned	

Step 5 — Tools and Techniques for Resource Mapping

Effective mapping requires analytical and digital tools to transform data into strategy.

Core Tools

Tool	Purpose
GIS Mapping	Visualize natural, urban, and infrastructure assets
SWOT Analysis	Identify strengths, weaknesses, opportunities, threats
PESTEL Analysis	Assess external macroeconomic factors
Resource Flow Charts	Track input-output systems
Digital Dashboards	Centralize real-time data for decision-making

Step 6 — Business Canvas Application

Economic Resource Mapping Canvas

Block	Details
Value Proposition	Comprehensive understanding of assets to maximize productivity and revenue
Key Activities	Resource audits, capacity assessment, stakeholder engagement, risk analysis
Key Resources	Data repositories, experts, community volunteers
Key Partners	Universities, NGOs, private sector, government agencies
Revenue Streams	Monetized land, talent, cultural events, intellectual property
Customer Segments	Government planners, investors, entrepreneurs, citizens
Channels	Digital dashboards, stakeholder meetings, public reports
Customer Relationships	Transparent, participatory, trust-based
Cost Structure	Audit operations, IT systems, data collection
Metrics	Utilization ratio, gap closure index, participation rate, revenue from untapped resources

Step 7 — Policy and Strategy Recommendations

Policy Area	Strategic Recommendation
Resource Optimization	Incentivize maximum value extraction from all assets
Skill Development	Align workforce skills with high-growth industries
Investment Planning	Channel funding into underutilized sectors
Cultural Monetization	Develop ethical tourism and creative industries
Technology Deployment	Use GIS, dashboards, and digital platforms for monitoring

Step 8 — Implementation Timeline

Phase	Activities	Outcome
Phase 1 (0–6 months)	Resource inventory, stakeholder registry	Baseline understanding
Phase 2 (6–12 months)	Capacity assessment, gap analysis	Opportunity identification
Phase 3 (1–2 years)	Pilot revenue projects	Feasibility validation
Phase 4 (2–5 years)	Scale initiatives, integrate technology	Sustainable growth

Step 9 — Risk Mitigation and Sustainability

To ensure long-term success, resource mapping must include resilience planning.

Key Safeguards

- Integrate climate, economic, and social risk assessments
- Develop contingency plans for critical sectors
- Implement resource conservation and sustainability programs
- Protect cultural and environmental assets for future generations

Conclusion

Mapping resources and capabilities is the **foundation of all economic planning.**

When communities fully understand what they possess, they gain the power to:

- Maximize productivity and efficiency
- Unlock hidden economic opportunities
- Close critical gaps in revenue and skills
- Build a strong and sustainable path toward economic

sovereignty

Resource awareness is not just data—it is **strategic power**.

Chapter 3 — Building a Strategic Vision

Objective

A strategic vision transforms a community's or nation's resource inventory into a coherent roadmap for long-term growth and prosperity. Without a clear vision, resources remain fragmented and underutilized. With a strong vision, they become engines of sustainable economic, social, and cultural development.

This chapter enables leaders and institutions to:

- Translate resource mapping into actionable goals
- Define short-, medium-, and long-term objectives
- Align stakeholders around a shared prosperity agenda
- Develop tools, blueprints, and implementation frameworks

Why a Strategic Vision Matters

A well-defined strategic vision delivers four critical outcomes:

- **Direction** — Provides clarity for policymakers, investors, and citizens
- **Focus** — Ensures efficient deployment of limited resources
- **Accountability** — Establishes measurable targets and tracking mechanisms
- **Motivation** — Inspires engagement, trust, and collective action

Case Examples

- **Singapore** — Despite limited natural resources, a clear long-term vision for trade, education, and urban planning transformed it into a global economic powerhouse.
- **Marrakesh** — Leveraged cultural heritage and tourism

strategy to drive employment, revenue, and global visibility.

Lesson: Vision converts latent potential into measurable, sustainable outcomes.

Step 1 — Define Core Goals

Strategic goals should integrate economic, social, and cultural priorities.

Goal Categories

Category	Strategic Objectives
Economic Goals	Achieve self-sufficiency in essential sectors; expand local industries; reduce dependence on imports and aid
Social Goals	Improve employment and education; ensure equitable service access; strengthen community cohesion
Cultural Goals	Preserve heritage; monetize cultural assets; develop globally competitive creative industries

Step 2 — Set SMART Objectives

Each goal must be translated into measurable outcomes using the SMART framework (Specific, Measurable, Achievable, Relevant, Time-bound).

SMART Objectives Framework

Objective	Metric	Timeline	Responsible Stakeholder
Increase SME revenue	% growth in SME income	3 years	Economic Council, Chambers of Commerce
Reduce unemployment	% decrease in unemployment	5 years	Labor Ministry, NGOs
Develop cultural tourism	Annual visitors & revenue	3 years	Tourism Board, Cultural Department

Step 3 — Stakeholder Alignment

Sustainable vision requires alignment across all actors influencing development.

Stakeholder Influence Matrix

Influence Level	Stakeholders
High Influence / High Interest	City planners, investors, major institutions
High Influence / Low Interest	National authorities, regulators
Low Influence / High Interest	Entrepreneurs, citizens, youth groups

Engagement mechanisms should include **vision workshops, town halls, and structured consultations** to ensure collective ownership.

Stakeholder Alignment Checklist

Requirement	Status
Stakeholder map created	
Workshop schedule implemented	
Feedback integrated into vision	
Governance and accountability defined	

Step 4 — Strategic Planning Frameworks

SWOT Analysis

Element	Example
Strengths	Cultural assets, skilled workforce
Weaknesses	Infrastructure gaps, limited capital
Opportunities	Export markets, tourism, digital economy
Threats	Global shocks, climate change, instability

PESTEL Analysis

Factor	Focus Area
Political	Stability, regulatory frameworks
Economic	Market conditions, investment climate
Social	Demographics, education levels
Technological	ICT infrastructure, digital adoption
Environmental	Sustainability, climate risk
Legal	Property rights, compliance

Scenario Planning

Scenario	Description
Base Case	Gradual growth through optimization
Optimistic Case	Rapid development through investment
Pessimistic Case	External shocks or revenue disruptions

Step 5 — Develop the Strategic Blueprint

A complete strategic blueprint includes:

- **Vision Statement** — A clear and inspiring long-term direction (5–10 years)
- **Mission Statement** — The pathway to achieving the vision
- **Action Plan** — Initiatives, timelines, responsibilities, KPIs
- **Monitoring Framework** — Dashboards, reports, periodic evaluations

Conceptual Strategic Blueprint Structure

Vision: Self-sustaining, prosperous, and culturally vibrant communities

Core Pillars:

- Economic Initiatives — diversified revenue, industry growth
- Social Initiatives — employment, education, healthcare
- Cultural Initiatives — tourism, heritage preservation, creative economy

- Governance — transparency, participatory systems

Step 6 — Business Canvas Integration
Strategic Vision Canvas

Block	Details
Value Proposition	Long-term roadmap for economic, social, and cultural prosperity
Key Activities	Resource mapping, planning, policy design, stakeholder engagement
Key Resources	Experts, community leaders, digital systems
Key Partners	Government, NGOs, investors, private sector
Revenue Streams	Taxes, trade, tourism, cultural industries
Customer Segments	Citizens, investors, entrepreneurs, tourists
Channels	Digital platforms, policy documents, town halls
Customer Relationships	Transparent, participatory, trust-based
Cost Structure	Planning operations, data systems, engagement activities
Metrics	Goal achievement rate, satisfaction levels, revenue growth

Step 7 — Risk Assessment and Contingency Planning

Risk	Impact	Mitigation Strategy
Stakeholder misalignment	Medium	Continuous engagement and feedback loops
Resource shortfalls	High	Diversified income and reserve funds
Implementation delays	Medium	Clear timelines and accountability structures
External shocks	High	Scenario planning and contingency reserves

Step 8 — Implementation Timeline

Phase	Activities	Outcome
Phase 1 (0–6 months)	Vision workshops and stakeholder engagement	Shared direction
Phase 2 (6–12 months)	Define SMART objectives and KPIs	Measurable targets
Phase 3 (1–2 years)	Pilot initiatives	Test and refine
Phase 4 (2–5 years)	Scale initiatives and integrate systems	Sustainable growth
Phase 5 (5–10 years)	Full integration of all sectors	Economic sovereignty

Step 9 — Community Mindset and Culture

Economic transformation requires a shift in mindset and culture:

- Promote **collective ownership and accountability**
- Encourage **long-term thinking over short-term gains**
- Align development with **ethics, equity, and sustainability**
- Build trust through transparency and participation

A strong vision is sustained not just by policy—but by **people, values, and shared purpose.**

Conclusion

A strategic vision is the bridge between potential and prosperity.

By defining clear goals, aligning stakeholders, applying analytical frameworks, and implementing structured action plans, communities, cities, and nations can fully unlock the value of their resources.

A well-designed vision does not merely guide growth—it **mobilizes people, capital, and culture toward a shared future of dignity, resilience, and prosperity**

Chapter 4 — Revenue Generation Strategies

Objective

Revenue generation is the engine of prosperity. It enables communities, cities, and nations to finance development, strengthen autonomy, and invest in long-term growth.

This chapter provides a comprehensive roadmap to:

- Identify diverse, ethical, and culturally aligned revenue streams
- Develop structured, actionable strategies for implementation
- Create scalable blueprints and business canvas models
- Ensure revenue systems are sustainable, measurable, and resilient

Why Revenue Diversification Matters

Diversification is essential to long-term economic stability and independence.

It enables:

- **Risk Reduction** — No single income source dominates or creates vulnerability
- **Autonomy** — Communities finance their own development priorities
- **Growth Enablement** — Surplus revenue funds education, infrastructure, and innovation
- **Social Impact** — Revenue supports healthcare, education, and quality of life improvements

Case Examples

- **Malaysia** — Built a diversified halal economy combining exports, Islamic finance, and tourism
- **Istanbul** — Leveraged tourism, crafts, and heritage industries to generate local income and employment

Step 1 — Categorize Revenue Streams

A resilient economy draws from multiple revenue channels:

Revenue Categories

Category	Revenue Sources
Taxation & Local Levies	Property tax, income tax, business registration fees
Trade & Export Industries	Halal goods, textiles, tech services, artisanal products
Services & Tourism	Religious tourism, education, healthcare, hospitality
Investments & Endowments	Sovereign/community funds, venture capital, infrastructure investments
Cultural & Intellectual Property	Arts, crafts, music, literature, patents, trademarks

Step 2 — Strategic Implementation Blueprint

Phase-Based Revenue Strategy

Phase	Timeline	Key Actions	Outcome
Phase 1 — Immediate Boost	0–1 year	Audit revenue, formalize businesses, launch pilot projects	Quick revenue increase
Phase 2 — Diversification	1–3 years	Expand exports, develop tourism, invest in skills	Stable income streams
Phase 3 — Sustainability	3–10 years	Create funds, scale digital services, institutionalize cultural industries	Long-term fiscal independence

Step 3 — Revenue Planning Checklist

Task	Completed (✓/✗)	Notes
Existing revenue streams audited		
High-potential sectors identified		
Pilot projects launched		
Stakeholders engaged		
Policy incentives implemented		
Monitoring systems established		
Diversification targets defined		

Step 4 — Risk Management

Risk	Impact	Mitigation Strategy
Dependence on single sector	High	Diversify across multiple revenue streams
Policy instability	Medium	Multi-year policy frameworks and legal safeguards
Market fluctuations	High	Reserve funds and financial hedging
Community resistance	Medium	Transparent engagement and communication

Step 5 — Business Canvas Application

Revenue Generation Canvas

Block	Details
Value Proposition	Reliable, diversified, and culturally aligned revenue streams
Key Activities	Tax reform, trade facilitation, service development, investment management
Key Resources	Skilled workforce, cultural assets, capital reserves
Key Partners	Investors, government agencies, NGOs, trade organizations
Revenue Streams	Taxes, exports, tourism, services, investments
Customer Segments	Citizens, entrepreneurs, domestic and global investors
Channels	Policy frameworks, digital platforms, business forums
Customer Relationships	Transparent, participatory, community-centered
Cost Structure	Infrastructure, operations, service development
Metrics	Diversification index, ROI, tax compliance, cultural monetization

Step 6 — Tools and Techniques

Tool	Purpose
Market Feasibility Studies	Identify viable sectors for revenue generation
Cost-Benefit Analysis	Prioritize high-return initiatives
Digital Platforms	Enable e-commerce, service delivery, tourism promotion
Monitoring Dashboards	Track revenue, compliance, and sector performance

Step 7 — Policy Recommendations

Policy Area	Recommendation
Tax Reform	Introduce fair and efficient tax systems
SME Development	Incentivize small business registration and growth
Digital Economy	Invest in e-commerce and digital platforms
Cultural Economy	Monetize heritage while preserving identity
Investment Ecosystem	Create community funds and startup financing programs

Step 8 — Metrics for Monitoring Success

Metric	Target	Frequency
Revenue Diversification Ratio	5+ independent sources	Quarterly
SME Contribution to Local GDP	25% within 5 years	Annual
Tourism Revenue Growth	10–15% annually	Annual
Investment ROI	8–12% return	Annual
Cultural Asset Revenue	Defined annual target	Annual

Step 9 — Community Engagement and Economic Mindset

Revenue systems succeed when communities actively participate.

Key Principles

- Encourage entrepreneurship at all levels
- Promote ownership of local economic initiatives
- Engage citizens in decision-making processes
- Highlight success stories to build trust and momentum

A strong economic culture transforms revenue systems into **community-driven growth engines.**

Conclusion

Revenue generation is the practical engine of prosperity.

By diversifying income streams, optimizing resources, and implementing structured frameworks with measurable outcomes, communities and nations can:

- Achieve economic sovereignty
- Strengthen social and cultural development
- Build sustainable, self-reliant growth systems

A diversified and ethical revenue model ensures not just wealth—but **resilience, dignity, and long-term prosperity**.

Chapter 5 — Building a Strategic Vision

Objective

A strategic vision transforms resources into purposeful, measurable action. It sets a clear direction for economic growth, social welfare, and cultural preservation. By defining short-, medium-, and long-term goals, communities, cities, and nations can establish a cohesive plan for sustainable prosperity.

Why a Strategic Vision Matters

A well-defined strategic vision provides the foundation for long-term development and resilience.

It ensures:

- **Direction** — Clear guidance for policy, investment, and community initiatives
- **Alignment** — Economic, social, and cultural priorities reinforce each other
- **Measurement** — Progress is tracked through KPIs and performance benchmarks
- **Resilience** — Communities are prepared to adapt to economic, environmental, and social change

Illustrative Examples

- **Singapore** transformed from a resource-limited territory into a global trade hub through long-term strategic planning.
- **Kuala Lumpur** combined economic development with cultural tourism and education initiatives to maximize local potential.

Step 1 — Define Economic Goals

Strategic planning requires a phased approach to ensure steady and sustainable progress.

Economic Goals by Timeline

Timeline	Strategic Objectives
Short-Term (0–2 years)	Strengthen existing revenue sources; reduce external aid dependency by 10–20%; launch SME and startup pilot programs
Medium-Term (2–5 years)	Diversify revenue streams; integrate healthcare, education, and employment programs; promote cultural tourism and creative industries
Long-Term (5–10 years)	Achieve fiscal self-sufficiency; establish investment funds and endowments; institutionalize governance systems

Step 2 — Strategic Alignment

For a vision to succeed, economic goals must align with social and cultural priorities.

Alignment Framework

Area	Strategic Focus
Economic & Social Alignment	Employment programs, skill development, healthcare access
Economic & Cultural Alignment	Heritage tourism, arts, ethical business practices
Inclusivity	Ensure participation of citizens, businesses, and institutions

Checklist — Alignment Tasks

Task	Status
Vision statement drafted and approved	
KPIs defined for economic, social, and cultural goals	
Risk assessment completed	
Stakeholder engagement plan created	

Step 3 — Risk Assessment and Contingency Planning

Risk	Impact	Mitigation Strategy
Stakeholder misalignment	Medium	Workshops, participatory planning
Revenue shortfalls	High	Diversified income streams and reserve funds
Cultural asset degradation	Medium	Preservation policies and sustainable tourism
External economic shocks	High	Scenario planning and strategic reserves

Step 4 — Stakeholder Mapping and Engagement

Key Stakeholders

- Citizens and community members
- Investors and entrepreneurs
- Local businesses
- Government agencies
- Cultural and religious leaders

Engagement Strategies

Method	Purpose
Town hall meetings	Community dialogue and transparency
Online forums & surveys	Continuous feedback
Participatory budgeting	Citizen-led decision-making

Goal: Create shared ownership of the vision and commitment to its implementation.

Step 5 — Strategic Blueprint (5-Year Rolling Plan)

A rolling strategic plan ensures both long-term direction and flexibility.

5-Year Strategic Plan Framework

Year	Focus	Key Activities	Metrics
Year 1	Foundation	Resource mapping, stakeholder alignment, pilot projects	Engagement rate, pilot ROI
Year 2	Expansion	Diversify revenue, launch social programs	Revenue diversification index, social impact
Year 3	Integration	Integrate economic and cultural initiatives	Integrated projects, tourism revenue
Year 4	Scaling	Expand investment and community participation	Investment growth, participation rate
Year 5	Evaluation	Review KPIs and refine strategy	Fiscal independence score, sustainability index

Note: Annual reviews ensure adaptability while maintaining long-term goals.

Step 6 — Business Canvas Application

Strategic Vision Business Canvas

Block	Details
Value Proposition	Sustainable, inclusive, and culturally aligned prosperity
Key Activities	Resource optimization, planning workshops, pilot projects, policy development
Key Resources	Human capital, cultural assets, financial reserves
Key Partners	Citizens, investors, government, cultural institutions
Revenue Streams	Trade, tourism, SMEs, services
Customer Segments	Citizens, investors, tourists, entrepreneurs
Channels	Policy frameworks, digital platforms, workshops
Customer Relationships	Transparent, participatory, trust-based
Cost Structure	Planning operations, engagement, monitoring systems
Metrics	KPI achievement, satisfaction, revenue growth, social and cultural impact

Step 7 — Monitoring and Evaluation

Performance Management Framework

Element	Approach
KPIs	Track economic, social, and cultural performance
Tools	Dashboards, digital reporting systems
Reviews	Annual strategic reviews and adjustments
Community Feedback	Public scorecards and participatory evaluations

Outcome: Continuous improvement and data-driven decision-making.

Step 8 — Implementation Mindset

A strategic vision succeeds when supported by a strong collective mindset.

Core Principles

- Promote **participatory culture** where citizens are co-creators
- Encourage **long-term thinking** over short-term gains
- Embed **ethical values, social welfare, and cultural preservation** into economic planning
- Foster accountability and transparency across institutions

Conclusion

A strategic vision is the bridge between potential and prosperity.

By defining clear goals, aligning stakeholders, managing risks, and implementing structured blueprints, communities can transform their resources and capabilities into a **self-sustaining and prosperous system**.

A strong vision does not merely guide development—it **unites people, resources, and purpose into a resilient pathway for long-term economic, social, and cultural success**

Chapter 6 — Governance as an Economic Enabler

Objective

Governance is the backbone of sustainable economic growth. Policies, transparency, and institutional efficiency are not just administrative tools—they are economic levers. This chapter explains how effective governance drives revenue generation, builds investor confidence, and accelerates community prosperity.

Why Governance Drives Economic Growth

- **Predictability:** Clear and stable policies reduce business risks and encourage long-term investment.
- **Efficiency:** Streamlined bureaucracy accelerates projects, lowers administrative costs, and improves service delivery.
- **Trust:** Transparency builds credibility with citizens, investors, and partners.
- **Innovation:** Strong institutions promote entrepreneurship, trade, and cultural industries.

Case Examples

- **Dubai**: E-governance systems and simplified business registration enabled rapid economic diversification and global competitiveness.
- **Malaysia**: Anti-corruption initiatives and clear policy frameworks attracted foreign investment and strengthened domestic entrepreneurship.

Step 1 — Core Governance Goals

1. **Policy Clarity**

Laws and regulations that encourage investment, entrepreneurship, and economic activity.

2. **Transparency**
   Open budgets, public reporting, and citizen participation in decision-making.
3. **Efficiency**
   Reduced red tape, digitized services, and faster administrative processes.
4. **Anti-Corruption Measures**
   Strong oversight, audits, and accountability mechanisms.
5. **Fiscal Incentives**
   Tax breaks, subsidies, and grants aligned with strategic sectors.

Step 2 — Strategic Governance Plan
Anti-Corruption Measures

- Establish independent anti-corruption commissions
- Implement anonymous whistleblower systems
- Enforce strict penalties for misconduct

Streamlined Bureaucracy

- Digitize services via e-governance platforms
- Consolidate overlapping departments
- Set time-bound standards for permits and approvals

Fiscal Incentives

- Provide tax incentives for SMEs and startups
- Offer grants for cultural and social enterprises
- Develop public-private partnership (PPP) frameworks

Step 3 — Governance Checklist

Task	Completed (✓/✗)	Notes
Policy audit conducted		
Institutional efficiency assessment		
Anti-corruption measures implemented		
Tax compliance frameworks established		
E-governance portals operational		
Governance dashboard created		
Citizen feedback mechanisms in place		

Step 4 — Blueprint for Governance

Governance Dashboard

Purpose:

Real-time monitoring of policy compliance, fiscal performance, project timelines, and institutional efficiency.

Core Components

- Policy tracker (laws, updates, regulations)
- Revenue dashboard (tax collection, incentives, trade revenue)
- Compliance tracker (audits, permits, corruption cases)
- Citizen engagement interface (feedback and grievance systems)

Governance Dashboard

Policy Updates	Audit Status
Revenue Metrics	Tax Compliance
Project Timelines	Citizen Feedback

Step 5 — Business Canvas Application

Block	Details
Value Proposition	Transparent, efficient, accountable governance that drives economic growth
Key Activities	Policy drafting, audits, fiscal incentives, anti-corruption enforcement
Key Resources	Institutions, IT systems, legal frameworks, human capital
Key Partners	Citizens, investors, civil society, NGOs
Revenue Streams	Tax compliance, investments, business registrations
Customer Segments	Citizens, businesses, investors, community organizations
Channels	E-governance portals, dashboards, town halls, workshops
Customer Relationships	Participatory, transparent, accountable
Cost Structure	IT systems, audits, training, policy implementation
Metrics	Compliance rate, satisfaction, corruption reduction, efficiency KPIs

Step 6 — Monitoring and Evaluation

Key Performance Indicators (KPIs)

- Time required for business registration and permits
- Tax collection efficiency
- Number of corruption cases reported and resolved
- Citizen engagement and satisfaction scores
- Investment approvals and implementation rate

Tools

- Digital dashboards
- Quarterly audits

- Annual governance reports
- Citizen surveys and feedback loops

Step 7 — Risk Mitigation

Risk	Impact	Mitigation
Policy inconsistency	High	Legal review committees, annual policy updates
Institutional resistance	Medium	Change management, training programs
Low citizen engagement	Medium	Public awareness and participation incentives
Corruption recurrence	High	Independent oversight and strict penalties

Step 8 — Implementation Timeline

Phase	Activities	Outcome
Phase 1 (0–6 months)	Policy review, institutional audit, launch e-governance	Baseline governance metrics
Phase 2 (6–12 months)	Fiscal incentives, anti-corruption enforcement, streamlined bureaucracy	Increased efficiency and compliance
Phase 3 (1–3 years)	Dashboard monitoring, policy refinement, citizen engagement	Sustainable transparency
Phase 4 (3–5 years)	Scaling and integration with social and cultural policy	Full governance as an economic enabler

Step 9 — Community Mindset and Cultural Integration

- Promote ethical governance aligned with cultural and religious values
- Encourage citizen participation in oversight and decision-

making
- Embed accountability and long-term thinking into institutional culture

Conclusion

Effective governance is more than administration—it is a catalyst for economic, social, and cultural prosperity. By implementing transparent policies, anti-corruption systems, efficient bureaucracy, and targeted fiscal incentives, communities and nations can:

- Maximize resource utilization
- Build investor and citizen trust
- Increase revenue sustainability
- Foster innovation and long-term growth

Governance, when structured strategically, becomes a powerful engine for inclusive and resilient economic development.

Chapter 7 — Community Engagement and Stakeholder Mapping

Objective

Community engagement is the lifeblood of sustainable prosperity. True growth occurs when citizens, businesses, NGOs, and religious institutions actively participate in shaping the economic, social, and cultural direction of their community. This chapter provides a structured approach to mapping stakeholders, building trust, and creating participatory decision-making systems.

Why Community Engagement Matters

- **Ownership:** Citizens who participate feel invested in community success.
- **Transparency:** Open decision-making reduces corruption and misuse of resources.
- **Resource Optimization:** Businesses, NGOs, and institutions contribute expertise, networks, and capital.
- **Innovation:** Collective insights generate creative solutions for local challenges.

Case Examples

- **Portland, Oregon**: Participatory budgeting allowed citizens to directly allocate municipal funds, leading to targeted and impactful community improvements.
- **Islamic Waqf Boards:** Community-managed religious and charitable endowments ensured long-term sustainability and accountability.

Step 1 — Identify Stakeholders

Categories of Stakeholders

- **Citizens:** Local households, youth, women's groups
- **Businesses:** SMEs, cooperatives, trade associations, startups
- **NGOs & Civil Society:** Education, healthcare, environmental organizations
- **Religious Institutions:** Mosques, madrasas, community trusts
- **Government Bodies:** Municipal authorities, economic councils, regulators

Checklist — Stakeholder Mapping

- Stakeholder registry created
- Influence and interest levels assessed (high / medium / low)
- Potential contributions and resources identified
- Engagement preferences documented

Step 2 — Engagement Strategy

Goal: Build participatory systems where stakeholders shape decisions, budgets, and projects.

Core Methods

- **Participatory Budgeting:** Citizens propose and vote on development projects
- **Decision-Making Councils:** Multi-sector councils define priorities
- **Digital Platforms:** Online dashboards, apps, and forums for feedback
- **Town Halls & Community Meetings:** In-person transparency and dialogue
- **Surveys and Polls:** Data-driven decision support

Checklist — Engagement Strategy

- Participatory budgeting framework established
- Representative councils formed
- Digital engagement platforms launched
- Community feedback calendar created

Step 3 — Blueprint: Community Prosperity Board

Purpose

Integrate all sectors to coordinate projects, policies, and investments efficiently.

Structure

- **Chair:** Community leader or elected official
- **Members:** Citizens, businesses, NGOs, religious institutions, municipal bodies
- **Committees:**
    - Finance & Investment
    - Social Welfare & Education
    - Cultural & Heritage
    - Urban Planning & Infrastructure

Key Responsibilities

- Consolidate stakeholder input
- Prioritize projects based on economic, social, and cultural impact
- Monitor implementation
- Report progress transparently

```
Community Prosperity Board
├── Finance & Investment Committee
├── Social Welfare & Education Committee
```

├─ Cultural & Heritage Committee
└─ Urban Planning & Infrastructure Committee

Step 4 — Business Canvas Application

Block	Details
Value Proposition	Engaged, informed, empowered community driving inclusive prosperity
Key Activities	Stakeholder mapping, participatory budgeting, council meetings, feedback collection
Key Resources	Citizens, NGOs, businesses, religious institutions, digital platforms
Key Partners	Government, civil society, private sector, faith-based organizations
Revenue Streams	Community projects, crowd funding, grants, local taxes
Customer Segments	Citizens, entrepreneurs, NGOs, investors, cultural institutions
Channels	Town halls, workshops, forums, mobile apps
Customer Relationships	Participatory, transparent, trust-based
Cost Structure	Council operations, engagement campaigns, technology platforms
Metrics	Participation rate, project completion, satisfaction, engagement quality

Step 5 — Feedback Loops and Continuous Improvement Process Cycle

1. **Collect Feedback:** Surveys, town halls, digital platforms
2. **Analyze & Integrate:** Evaluate impact on economic, social, and cultural outcomes
3. **Respond & Communicate:** Show stakeholders how their input influenced decisions

4. **Iterate:** Update strategies based on real-world results

Checklist — Feedback Loops

- Digital and in-person channels active
- Feedback reviewed monthly
- Action plans communicated quarterly
- Continuous improvement metrics tracked

Step 6 — Risk Assessment & Mitigation

Risk	Impact	Mitigation
Low participation	Medium	Awareness campaigns, incentives
Unequal representation	High	Inclusive council composition
Conflict of interest	Medium	Codes of conduct, transparency
Stakeholder fatigue	Medium	Rotate roles, celebrate milestones

Step 7 — Implementation Timeline

Phase	Activities	Outcome
Phase 1 (0–3 months)	Stakeholder mapping and initial meetings	Engagement foundation
Phase 2 (3–6 months)	Councils formed, participatory budgeting launched	Inclusive decision-making
Phase 3 (6–12 months)	Digital platforms, town halls, feedback systems	Active engagement
Phase 4 (1–3 years)	Evaluate and refine structures, expand participation	Sustained trust and collaboration

Step 8 — Cultural Integration

- Embed values of **consultation (Shura)** and accountability
- Encourage community pride through inclusive planning
- Recognize contributions of citizens, institutions, and businesses

Conclusion

Engaged communities are prosperous communities.

By mapping stakeholders, creating participatory councils, integrating digital and in-person engagement, and continuously refining strategies:

- Citizens, businesses, NGOs, and religious institutions become **co-creators of prosperity**
- Resources are allocated efficiently and transparently
- Communities build resilience, trust, and accountability

Community engagement transforms governance from a top-down system into a shared, participatory engine for sustainable development.

Chapter 8 — Trade and Export Strategy

Objective

Trade and exports are pillars of national revenue and economic sovereignty. This chapter provides a comprehensive roadmap for Muslim nations, regions, and cities to generate revenue by leveraging culturally aligned products, technology, and strategic partnerships while expanding into international markets.

Why Trade and Exports Matter

- **Revenue Generation:** Exports bring in foreign currency and reduce trade deficits
- **Economic Diversification:** Moves economies beyond domestic consumption
- **Global Visibility:** Positions the nation as a competitive global player
- **Job Creation:** Stimulates manufacturing, logistics, services, and innovation

Case Examples

- **Turkey** — Expanded textile exports through international trade missions and global exhibitions
- **Malaysia** — Leveraged halal food and Islamic finance exports to capture global Muslim markets
- **Pakistan** — Developed IT and software outsourcing exports to global clients

Step 1 — Identify Export Sectors
Primary Focus Sectors

1. **Halal Products**

Food, pharmaceuticals, cosmetics, logistics certified under halal standards

2. **Textiles & Apparel**
   Traditional fabrics, garments, modest fashion, culturally inspired design
3. **Technology Exports**
   Software development, fin tech, SaaS platforms, outsourcing services
4. **Crafts & Cultural Goods**
   Handicrafts, artisanal goods, design products, cultural artifacts

Checklist — Sector Readiness Assessment

- Market demand analysis completed
- Production capacity reviewed
- Halal or international quality certifications obtained
- Logistics and supply chain feasibility assessed

Step 2 — Strategic Trade Approach

Core Strategy

Create a structured, incentivized ecosystem to support export growth.

Key Mechanisms

1. International Trade Missions

- Government-led delegations to key markets
- Partnerships with foreign distributors and trade chambers

2. Free Trade Agreements (FTAs)

- Preferential tariffs and quotas
- Alignment with priority export sectors

3. Export Incentives

- Tax exemptions and rebates
- Subsidies and export financing
- Grants for SMEs to achieve compliance and certification

4. Digital Export Platforms

- E-commerce marketplaces for global buyers
- Block chain-enabled supply chain verification for authenticity and trust

Step 3 — Export Readiness Checklist

Task	Completed	Notes
Product suitability assessed		
Halal/quality certifications obtained		
Production capacity verified		
Logistics & warehousing systems in place		
Customs & trade compliance completed		
Market intelligence & competitor analysis		
Trade mission plans drafted		

Step 4 — National Export Promotion Blueprint

National Export Promotion Agency (NEPA)

Purpose: Centralized body coordinating all export activities

Structure

```
National Export Promotion Agency
├── Halal Products Cell
├── Textile & Apparel Cell
├── Technology & IT Cell
└── Cultural & Crafts Cell
```

Core Functions

- Export strategy planning
- Certification and compliance support
- Market intelligence and research
- Investor and partner coordination
- Trade fairs and B2B matchmaking

Operational Highlights

- Export readiness certification programs
- Trade facilitation (logistics, finance, documentation)
- SME export onboarding programs

Step 5 — Business Canvas Application

Block	Details
Value Proposition	High-quality, culturally aligned export products
Key Activities	Export strategy, compliance, trade missions, marketing
Key Resources	Skilled workforce, production capacity, certifications
Key Partners	Trade bodies, distributors, logistics firms, governments
Revenue Streams	Export revenue, commissions, facilitation service fees
Customer Segments	International buyers, retail chains, distributors
Channels	Trade fairs, digital marketplaces, B2B platforms
Customer Relationships	Long-term, trust-based partnerships
Cost Structure	Certification, logistics, marketing, staffing
Metrics	Export growth rate, market penetration, compliance score

Step 6 — Risk Assessment & Mitigation

Risk	Impact	Mitigation
Market volatility	High	Diversify export destinations
Compliance failure	High	Certification training and audits
Logistics disruption	Medium	Multiple supply chain partners
Trade barriers	Medium	Diplomatic channels and FTAs

Step 7 — Implementation Timeline

Phase	Activities	Outcome
Phase 1 (0–6 months)	Sector identification, readiness assessment	Export roadmap defined
Phase 2 (6–12 months)	Establish NEPA, certify products, launch missions	Market access achieved
Phase 3 (1–3 years)	Expand digital exports, secure FTAs	Increased export volume
Phase 4 (3–5 years)	Diversify products, optimize strategy	Sustainable export economy

Step 8 — Cultural and Community Integration

- Align export strategy with **Islamic ethical business principles**
- Use cultural identity and storytelling as a **branding advantage**
- Engage artisans, SMEs, and youth in export ecosystems
- Promote inclusive growth across regions and communities

Conclusion

Trade and exports are powerful levers of prosperity and independence.

By:

- Prioritizing halal, textile, technology, and cultural sectors
- Establishing a centralized export promotion agency

- Leveraging FTAs, trade missions, and export incentives
- Using digital platforms and measurable KPIs

Nations, cities, and communities can build **diversified, sustainable, and globally competitive economies**—generating revenue while preserving cultural identity and social values

Chapter 9 — Tourism and Cultural Economy

Objective

Tourism is both a cultural and economic driver. Religious pilgrimages, heritage sites, festivals, and cultural experiences generate direct revenue, employment, and global recognition. This chapter outlines how Muslim nations, states, and cities can leverage culture and faith-based tourism to create sustainable economic growth while preserving identity.

Why Tourism Matters

- **Revenue Generation:** Entrance fees, hospitality, transport, and cultural products
- **Employment:** Jobs in hotels, guides, transportation, cultural performances, and retail
- **Cultural Preservation:** Heritage and religious sites are maintained and celebrated
- **Global Branding:** Positions cities and nations as culturally vibrant and authentic destinations

Case Examples

- **Mecca and Medina** — Pilgrimage tourism generates billions annually, supporting infrastructure and local economies
- **Istanbul** — Integrated heritage tourism combining museums, mosques, and cultural districts
- **Marrakesh** — Markets, festivals, and historic districts drive employment and local income

Step 1 — Identify Tourism Opportunities

Key Focus Areas

1. Religious Pilgrimage

- Mosques, Islamic heritage sites, Sufi shrines
- Pilgrimage routes and guided spiritual tours

2. Heritage Tourism

- Forts, palaces, ancient markets, historic neighborhoods

3. Festivals & Cultural Events

- Religious festivals
- Arts, handicrafts, music, literature events

4. Culinary Tourism

- Local cuisine and halal dining experiences

5. Experiential Tourism

- Workshops, storytelling tours, cultural immersion programs

Checklist — Tourism Readiness Assessment

- Accessibility (roads, airports, public transport)
- Accommodation capacity (hotels, guesthouses, lodges)
- Availability of multilingual guides
- Safety and security measures
- Strong digital presence and online booking

Step 2 — Strategic Tourism Development

Integrated Development Strategy

Infrastructure Development

- Pilgrimage facilities (lodging, sanitation, medical services)
- Restoration and maintenance of heritage sites
- Transport connectivity and signage

Cultural Tourism Packages

- Combined religious + historical + cultural tours
- Annual festival calendars aligned with global travel seasons
- Culinary and craft workshops

Digital Promotion

- Interactive websites, mobile apps, and virtual tours
- Social media campaigns targeting domestic and international visitors
- Online booking systems for tours, hotels, and events

Sustainability Measures

- Eco-friendly transport systems
- Waste management and environmental protection
- Training local communities in sustainable tourism practices

Step 3 — Tourism Master Plan Blueprint

Purpose

Create an integrated roadmap for tourism-led economic development.

Structure

```
Tourism Master Plan
      ├── Infrastructure Development
      ├── Marketing & Promotions
      ├── Cultural Preservation & Festivals
      ├── Local Economic Integration
      └── Sustainability & Monitoring
```

Key Components

- **Infrastructure:** Transport, accommodation, signage, safety, sanitation
- **Marketing:** Digital campaigns, international partnerships, travel expos
- **Cultural Preservation:** Site restoration, heritage laws, festival planning
- **Economic Integration:** Linking tourism to SMEs, artisans, and local businesses
- **Monitoring:** Visitor metrics, satisfaction surveys, environmental impact tracking

Step 4 — Business Canvas Application

Block	Details
Value Proposition	Authentic, safe, and immersive cultural and religious tourism experiences
Key Activities	Pilgrimage services, guided tours, festivals, marketing
Key Resources	Heritage sites, religious institutions, cultural assets, trained workforce
Key Partners	Hotels, tour operators, NGOs, cultural institutions
Revenue Streams	Entry fees, accommodation, tours, merchandise, festival tickets
Customer Segments	Pilgrims, domestic tourists, international travelers
Channels	Websites, travel apps, agencies, social media
Customer Relationships	Respectful, participatory, culturally sensitive
Cost Structure	Maintenance, staffing, marketing, digital platforms
Metrics	Tourist arrivals, revenue, satisfaction, repeat visits

Step 5 — Risk Assessment & Mitigation

Risk	Impact	Mitigation
Safety incidents	High	Security protocols and emergency response systems
Cultural degradation	Medium	Preservation laws and awareness campaigns
Seasonal demand fluctuations	Medium	Diversified tourism offerings and staggered festivals
Weak digital marketing	Medium	Professional marketing agencies and analytics

Step 6 — Implementation Timeline

Phase	Activities	Outcome
Phase 1 (0–6 months)	Readiness assessment, stakeholder mapping, digital launch	Visibility and baseline systems
Phase 2 (6–12 months)	Infrastructure upgrades, pilot tourism packages	Improved visitor experience
Phase 3 (1–3 years)	Full festival calendar, global promotion, community training	Increased tourist inflow
Phase 4 (3–5 years)	Sustainability integration, performance monitoring	Long-term growth and preservation

Step 7 — Community Integration and Cultural Preservation

- Train local residents as guides, artisans, and hospitality providers
- Ensure tourism respects religious practices and cultural norms
- Integrate local SMEs and craftspeople into tourism supply chains
- Celebrate heritage through storytelling, festivals, and exhibitions

Conclusion

Tourism and the cultural economy provide powerful pathways for prosperity while preserving identity and values.

By:

- Developing pilgrimage infrastructure and heritage

conservation
- Creating immersive and culturally aligned tourism experiences
- Leveraging digital promotion and sustainable practices
- Implementing a comprehensive Tourism Master Plan

Muslim nations, cities, and communities can achieve **economic growth, global recognition, and cultural resilience**—while ensuring that development remains ethical, inclusive, and rooted in heritage.

Chapter 10 — Energy and Natural Resources

Objective

Energy and natural resources are critical levers for national prosperity. Proper optimization of renewable and conventional energy not only generates revenue but also ensures sustainable development, environmental resilience, and industrial growth. This chapter provides a comprehensive roadmap for leveraging energy and resources effectively.

Why Energy and Resources Matter

- **Revenue Generation:** Energy sales, carbon credits, and resource-based industries
- **Industrial Growth:** Reliable energy supports manufacturing, technology, and services
- **Employment:** Jobs in construction, operations, maintenance, and engineering
- **Sustainability:** Reduced dependence on imports and improved climate resilience

Case Examples

- **Morocco** — Noor Solar Complex drives energy independence and export potential
- **Turkey** — Wind and geothermal projects diversify national energy mix
- **Malaysia** — Bioenergy integrated with agriculture maximizes renewable output

Step 1 — Map Energy and Resource Opportunities

Core Focus Areas

Renewable Energy

- Solar farms
- Wind parks
- Bioenergy from agricultural and urban waste
- Small-scale hydropower

Conventional Energy

- Efficient oil, gas, and coal use with emissions controls

Water Resources

- Irrigation, urban supply, industrial water systems

Minerals and Raw Materials

- Sustainable extraction and value-added processing

Energy Efficiency

- Smart grids
- Industrial audits
- Public conservation programs

Checklist — Resource Assessment

- Energy production capacity mapped
- Renewable resource availability analyzed (solar, wind,

biomass)
- Energy demand forecasted (industrial, commercial, residential)
- Grid efficiency evaluated
- Environmental impact assessments completed

Step 2 — Strategic Energy Approach

Integrated Energy Strategy

Renewable Energy Parks

- Solar farms in high-irradiance regions
- Wind farms in coastal and elevated zones
- Bioenergy facilities using agricultural and urban organic waste

Resource Efficiency Programs

- Energy audits for industries and municipalities
- Incentives for energy-efficient equipment
- Smart meters and real-time consumption tracking

Public-Private Partnerships (PPPs)

- Joint ventures for power generation and distribution
- Private investment in grid modernization
- Renewable technology R&D collaborations

Policy Support

- Tax incentives for renewable energy investments

- Feed-in tariffs for small-scale producers
- Carbon credit markets and green certification programs

Step 3 — Energy Project Checklist

Task	Completed (✓/✗)	Notes
Resource mapping completed		
Energy audits conducted		
Feasibility studies (solar, wind, bioenergy)		
PPP agreements negotiated		
Grid modernization plan drafted		
Environmental & social impact assessments		
Regulatory compliance ensured		

Step 4 — Blueprint: National Energy Grid Modernization Plan

Purpose

Integrate renewable and conventional energy into a resilient, efficient, and intelligent grid.

Core Components

```
National Energy Grid
    ├── Renewable Generation (Solar, Wind, Bio)
    ├── Conventional Energy (Gas, Coal, Hydro)
    ├── Storage & Smart Grid Systems
    ├── Industrial & Residential Distribution
    └── Monitoring & Analytics Platforms
```

Key Elements

- **Generation Mix:** Balanced renewable + conventional

sources

- **Distribution Network:** Smart grid with reduced transmission losses
- **Energy Storage:** Batteries, pumped hydro, thermal storage
- **Monitoring Systems:** Real-time production and consumption tracking
- **Community Micro-grids:** Local energy systems for villages and neighborhoods

Step 5 — Business Canvas Application

Block	Details
Value Proposition	Reliable, affordable, and sustainable energy for all sectors
Key Activities	Energy generation, grid modernization, efficiency programs
Key Resources	Solar/wind parks, power plants, smart grid infrastructure, skilled workforce
Key Partners	Energy companies, investors, municipalities, technology providers
Revenue Streams	Electricity sales, carbon credits, PPP dividends, green incentives
Customer Segments	Households, SMEs, industries, government institutions
Channels	Grid networks, Micro-grids, digital monitoring platforms
Customer Relationships	Reliable service, transparent billing, responsive support
Cost Structure	Infrastructure, maintenance, R&D, regulatory compliance
Metrics	Renewable share %, grid uptime, energy efficiency, revenue growth

Step 6 — Risk Assessment & Mitigation

Risk	Impact	Mitigation
Intermittent renewable supply	High	Hybrid energy mix and storage systems
Infrastructure damage	High	Disaster-resilient design, redundancy, insurance
Regulatory delays	Medium	Fast-track approvals, policy alignment
Investment shortfalls	Medium	PPPs, green bonds, international financing
Environmental degradation	Medium	Strict EIA compliance, sustainable extraction

Step 7 — Implementation Timeline

Phase	Activities	Outcome
Phase 1 (0–6 months)	Resource mapping, feasibility studies, PPP setup	Baseline assessment
Phase 2 (6–12 months)	Pilot renewable projects and energy audits	Initial efficiency and revenue gains
Phase 3 (1–3 years)	Scale renewable parks and smart grid deployment	Diversified energy ecosystem
Phase 4 (3–5 years)	Integrate carbon markets and advanced analytics	Sustainable, resilient energy economy

Step 8 — Community and Cultural Integration

- Train local workforce in renewable energy installation and maintenance
- Educate citizens on conservation and energy efficiency
- Encourage community-owned micro-grid projects

- Align energy stewardship with Islamic values of **Khilafah** (responsible guardianship of resources)

Conclusion

Energy and natural resources are both a strategic asset and a powerful revenue engine.

By:

- Expanding solar, wind, bioenergy, and efficient conventional energy
- Modernizing grids and improving efficiency
- Encouraging public-private investment partnerships
- Leveraging revenue from energy sales, carbon credits, and industrial growth

Muslim nations, cities, and communities can achieve **economic resilience, environmental sustainability, and long-term prosperity**—building an energy system that supports both development and ethical stewardship of resources.

Chapter 11 — Digital Economy and Innovation Hubs

Objective

The digital economy is the engine of modern economic growth. Establishing fin tech zones, AI labs, and startup incubators enables Muslim nations, cities, and communities to generate revenue, foster entrepreneurship, and position themselves as global leaders in innovation.

Why the Digital Economy Matters

1. Revenue Generation

- Fin tech services
- AI-powered products
- E-commerce platforms
- Digital payments
- Intellectual property (IP) commercialization

2. Employment Creation

- High-tech jobs
- Startup ecosystems
- Gig economy expansion

3. Global Competitiveness

- Attract foreign investment
- Export digital services
- Build international partnerships

4. Cultural and Social Impact

- Technology solutions tailored to community needs
- Ethical AI aligned with Islamic values
- Digital inclusion for underserved populations

Case Examples

- **Cyberjaya (Malaysia)**
  A successful digital city integrating IT companies, startups, and education institutions.
- **Dubai Internet City (UAE)**
  A tax-free innovation hub attracting global technology firms.
- **Pakistan Tech Incubators**
  Provide mentorship, seed funding, and AI labs for young innovators.

Step 1 — Identify Digital Opportunities
Core Focus Areas

- **Fin tech Zones**: Mobile banking, payment gateways, Islamic finance solutions
- **AI & Data Labs**: Machine learning, predictive analytics, automation
- **Startup Incubators & Accelerators**: Mentorship, funding, networking
- **Digital Services**: E-commerce, edtech, health tech, logistics
- **IP-Driven Products**: Software, AI tools, Block chain solutions

Digital Readiness Checklist

- Startup registry established
- Technology infrastructure audit completed

- Funding pipelines identified
- IP and patent frameworks reviewed
- Skilled talent pool available

Step 2 — Strategic Approach
Policy Incentives

- Tax holidays for digital startups
- Reduced import duties on tech hardware
- R&D grant programs

Mentorship & Incubation

- University and global tech partnerships
- Access to experienced founders
- Structured startup scaling programs

IP Protection Framework

- Simplified patent registration
- Copyright and trademark protection
- Cyber security standards

Infrastructure Development

- Co-working spaces and innovation labs
- High-speed internet and cloud computing
- Data centers for analytics

Market Access

- Government-backed e-commerce portals
- International tech fairs
- Global digital marketplaces

Step 3 — National Digital Innovation Board

Purpose

Coordinate and scale national digital economy initiatives.

Structure

- **Chair**: Minister of Technology or Economic Development
- **Members**: Entrepreneurs, investors, academics, government officials

Committees

- Fin tech
- AI & Data
- Startup Incubation
- Digital Infrastructure

Functions

- National innovation strategy
- Funding allocation
- IP governance
- Global partnerships

Step 4 — Business Canvas Application

Block	Details
Value Proposition	Innovation ecosystem for jobs and global competitiveness
Key Activities	R&D, incubation, mentorship, infrastructure
Key Resources	Talent, startups, AI labs, venture capital
Key Partners	Universities, investors, global tech firms
Revenue Streams	Equity, IP licensing, software, digital services
Customer Segments	Entrepreneurs, tech firms, global clients
Channels	Incubators, accelerators, online platforms
Customer Relationships	Mentorship and continuous engagement
Cost Structure	Infrastructure, funding, marketing
Metrics	Startup survival rate, jobs created, IP registrations

Step 5 — Risk Assessment & Mitigation

Risk	Impact	Mitigation
Talent shortage	High	Scholarships, coding boot camps
Regulatory delays	Medium	Simplified digital governance
Cyber security threats	High	National Cyber security standards
Funding gaps	Medium	Venture funds, global investors
Market adoption issues	Medium	Pilot programs, mentorship

Step 6 — Implementation Timeline

Phase	Activities	Outcome
0–6 Months	Infrastructure audit, startup registry, AI labs	Baseline readiness
6–12 Months	Launch incubators, fin tech zones	Operational ecosystem
1–3 Years	Scale accelerators, global partnerships	Job and revenue growth
3–5 Years	IP commercialization, global expansion	Sustainable digital economy

Step 7 — Community Integration

- Promote **youth and women participation** in tech startups
- Train entrepreneurs in **Islamic fin tech and ethical AI**
- Use innovation hubs to **solve local community challenges**

Implementation Mindset

- Foster **entrepreneurial culture**
- Encourage **long-term innovation thinking**
- Align technology with **ethical and cultural values**

Conclusion

Digital economy and innovation hubs are powerful engines of sustainable prosperity.

By:

- Building fin tech zones, AI labs, and incubators
- Providing policy incentives and IP protection
- Establishing a National Digital Innovation Board
- Connecting innovation with community and culture

Communities can create **globally competitive, self-sustaining digital economies** that generate wealth, jobs, and social impact for generations to come.

Chapter 12 — Taxation and Revenue Management Systems

Objective

Modern, fair, and efficient taxation systems are the backbone of national revenue. A well-designed fiscal framework ensures sustainable funding for public services, infrastructure, and social welfare, while strengthening transparency, accountability, and public trust.

Why Taxation Matters

1. Revenue Generation

- Funds infrastructure, healthcare, education, and social programs
- Supports public services and national development

2. Economic Equity

- Progressive taxation reduces inequality
- Ensures fair contribution based on income and capacity

3. Trust and Compliance

- Transparent systems increase voluntary compliance
- Strengthens citizen-government trust

4. Investment and Growth

- Efficient taxation attracts investors
- Supports businesses and economic expansion

Case Examples

- **Malaysia**

Digital tax administration increased compliance and improved revenue collection.

- **United Arab Emirates (UAE)**
  VAT implementation with clear business guidelines ensured high compliance rates.
- **Turkey**
  Progressive tax reforms and modern auditing strengthened fiscal stability.

Step 1 — Define Tax Strategy
Core Focus Areas

- **Digital Tax Administration**
  Online filing, e-payments, automated compliance systems
- **Progressive Tax Structures**
  Fair taxation on individuals and corporates
  Exemptions and incentives for SMEs
- **Revenue Diversification**
  Income tax, corporate tax, VAT, property tax, environmental levies
- **Taxpayer Education**
  Awareness programs to improve voluntary compliance
- **Audit & Compliance Systems**
  Risk-based audits, automated monitoring, dispute resolution

Tax Readiness Checklist

- Tax base analyzed
- Digital infrastructure established
- Progressive tax policies drafted
- Compliance systems in place
- Taxpayer education programs designed

Step 2 — Strategic Implementation
Strategy
Create a modern, integrated, and accountable taxation system.
Digital Tax Administration

- Secure e-filing portals
- Online payment gateways
- AI-based fraud detection systems

Progressive Tax Structures

- Rates linked to income and business size
- SME exemptions and incentives
- Tax benefits for green energy and social enterprises

Central Revenue Monitoring

- Real-time dashboards
- Integrated national and local systems
- Automated compliance notifications

Taxpayer Engagement

- Multilingual guides and helplines
- Community education workshops
- Regular public transparency reports

Step 3 — Central Revenue Monitoring System
Purpose
Provide real-time tracking, analytics, and accountability for public revenue systems.
Core Components

- **Dashboard:** Revenue by sector, region, and category
- **Analytics Module:** Predict trends and compliance risks
- **Integration Layer:** Connect government, banks, and businesses
- **Transparency Portal:** Public access to revenue insights

System Structure

Central Revenue Monitoring Dashboard
├─ Digital Filing & Payments
├─ Compliance & Audit Analytics
├─ Revenue Tracking by Sector
├─ Citizen Transparency Portal
└─ Policy & Strategy Insights

Step 4 — Business Canvas Application

Block	Details
Value Proposition	Fair, transparent, and efficient revenue collection
Key Activities	Tax administration, monitoring, education, analytics
Key Resources	IT systems, auditors, legal frameworks
Key Partners	Banks, businesses, government agencies
Revenue Streams	Income tax, corporate tax, VAT, property tax
Customer Segments	Citizens, businesses, institutions
Channels	Digital portals, mobile apps, tax offices
Customer Relationships	Transparent, service-oriented, participatory
Cost Structure	IT systems, audits, training, communication
Metrics	Compliance rate, revenue growth, satisfaction

Step 5 — Risk Assessment & Mitigation

Risk	Impact	Mitigation
Tax evasion	High	Digital monitoring, audits, penalties
Cyber security threats	High	Encryption, system audits, secure portals
Public mistrust	Medium	Transparency campaigns, open reporting
Implementation delays	Medium	Phased rollout strategy
SME compliance complexity	Medium	Simplified filing, exemptions

Step 6 — Implementation Timeline

Phase	Activities	Outcome
0–6 Months	Portal setup, infrastructure audit, policy review	Operational baseline
6–12 Months	Progressive tax rollout, education programs	Higher compliance
1–3 Years	Real-time dashboards, automated audits	Optimized revenue
3–5 Years	AI analytics, full system automation	Modern tax ecosystem

Step 7 — Community Integration

- Promote **voluntary compliance culture**
- Educate citizens on **tax benefits and public spending**
- Support SMEs through **simplified tax frameworks**
- Encourage formalization of informal businesses

Implementation Mindset

- **Transparency first** — open reporting builds trust
- **Fairness and equity** — progressive taxation systems

- **Digital efficiency** — reduce bureaucracy and leakage
- **Community partnership** — citizens as stakeholders

Conclusion

Taxation and revenue management systems are foundational pillars of sustainable prosperity.

By:

- Implementing **digital, progressive, and transparent taxation**
- Building a **Central Revenue Monitoring System**
- Engaging citizens and businesses in compliance
- Linking fiscal systems to social welfare and economic growth

Muslim nations, cities, and communities can achieve **fiscal independence, economic justice, and long-term resilience**.

Chapter 13 — Industrial Clusters and Special Economic Zones

Objective

Industrial clusters and Special Economic Zones (SEZs) are powerful engines of state-level economic growth. By concentrating manufacturing, logistics, and export-oriented industries in well-planned zones, governments can boost revenue, generate employment, attract investment, and enhance global competitiveness.

Why Industrial Clusters and SEZs Matter

1. Revenue Generation

- Corporate taxes, export duties, and service fees
- Industrial utilities and logistics revenues

2. Employment Creation

- Manufacturing, logistics, administration, and support services
- High-volume job creation across skill levels

3. Investment Attraction

- Incentives draw domestic and foreign direct investment (FDI)
- Encourages long-term industrial partnerships

4. Regional Development

- Accelerates urbanization and infrastructure growth
- Strengthens local supply chains and skill development

Case Examples

- **Dubai Industrial City**
  A major hub for logistics, light manufacturing, and trade serving global markets.
- **Iskandar Development Region (Malaysia)**
  Integrated industrial clusters supporting exports, SMEs, and regional development.
- **Organized Industrial Zones (Turkey)**
  Strategically designed SEZs supporting export-led industrial growth.

Step 1 — Identify SEZ Opportunities
Focus Areas

- **Manufacturing Hubs:** automobiles, textiles, electronics, halal products
- **Logistics & Warehousing:** ports, railways, cold storage, distribution hubs
- **Export-Oriented Units:** goods tailored for regional and global markets
- **Innovation Industries:** tech manufacturing, green energy, pharmaceuticals
- **Support Services:** banking, legal, HR, training, and maintenance services

SEZ Readiness Checklist

- Land availability and zoning approval
- Infrastructure access (roads, power, water, internet)
- Skilled workforce availability
- Regulatory approvals and permits
- Supply chain and logistics mapping

Step 2 — Strategic Approach

Strategy

Develop **integrated, high-performance SEZ ecosystems** that maximize efficiency, investment inflow, and export competitiveness.

Tax & Incentive Framework

- Tax holidays (5–10 years)
- Reduced import/export duties
- Incentives tied to employment and export performance

Infrastructure Investment

- Industrial parks with utilities and transport access
- Logistics hubs with cold chains and freight systems
- Smart zones with digital management and monitoring

Skill Development Programs

- Vocational training and certification programs
- University and polytechnic partnerships
- Apprenticeships and on-the-job training

Governance & Regulatory Support

- Single-window clearance for permits
- E-governance compliance platforms
- Transparent land and contract systems

Cluster Development Strategy

- Group complementary industries for efficiency
- Shared R&D, utilities, and logistics
- Integrate local SMEs into supply chains

Step 3 — SEZ Development Master Plan

Purpose

Create a scalable, structured blueprint for long-term SEZ success.

Core Components

- **Land & Zoning:** industrial, commercial, and residential planning
- **Infrastructure:** roads, ports, power, IT, and waste systems
- **Investment Promotion:** marketing, investor outreach, FDI facilitation
- **Workforce Development:** training centers and education partnerships
- **Governance:** SEZ Authority for oversight and compliance

System Structure

```
SEZ Development Master Plan
├── Land & Zoning
├── Infrastructure Development
├── Investment Attraction
├── Workforce Development
└── Governance & Operations
```

Step 4 — Business Canvas Application

Block	Details
Value Proposition	Efficient, export-driven industrial ecosystems
Key Activities	Manufacturing, logistics, exports, training
Key Resources	Land, infrastructure, skilled workforce
Key Partners	Investors, manufacturers, universities, logistics firms
Revenue Streams	Corporate tax, export duties, utilities, services
Customer Segments	Domestic & foreign manufacturers, exporters
Channels	SEZ authority, trade bodies, industrial boards
Customer Relationships	Transparent governance, investor facilitation
Cost Structure	Infrastructure, training, operations, marketing
Metrics	Jobs created, export volume, output, investor satisfaction

Step 5 — Risk Assessment & Mitigation

Risk	Impact	Mitigation
Land acquisition disputes	High	Community engagement, fair compensation
Investor reluctance	Medium	Incentives, ease of doing business
Skill shortages	Medium	Training and apprenticeship programs
Infrastructure delays	High	Phased development and PPPs
Environmental impact	Medium	Strict EIA and sustainable practices

Step 6 — Implementation Timeline

Phase	Activities	Outcome
0–6 Months	Land allocation, SEZ authority setup, feasibility studies	Investment-ready
6–12 Months	Infrastructure build-out, investor outreach	Operational pilot zones
1–3 Years	Cluster expansion, training programs	Scaled production & employment
3–5 Years	Export integration, R&D, optimization	Sustainable industrial growth

Step 7 — Community and Cultural Integration

- Integrate **local SMEs** into SEZ supply chains
- Train youth in **technical and managerial skills**
- Ensure development aligns with **cultural values and environmental sustainability**
- Promote **local entrepreneurship** in services like logistics, catering, and transport

Implementation Mindset

- **Export-first orientation**
- **Efficiency through clustering**
- **Investor-friendly governance**
- **Inclusive workforce development**
- **Sustainable and ethical industrialization**

Conclusion

Industrial clusters and SEZs are among the most powerful tools for **state-level economic transformation.**

By:

- Concentrating industries for efficiency and export readiness

- Offering fiscal incentives and business-friendly policies
- Integrating infrastructure, workforce, and logistics planning
- Linking revenue streams to production, exports, and services

Muslim states and cities can achieve **sustainable revenue growth, job creation, investment attraction, and global competitiveness**, while advancing inclusive socio-economic development.

Chapter 14 — Agriculture, Food Security, and Agri-Business

Objective

Agriculture is a cornerstone of state and local prosperity. By modernizing farming, ensuring food security, and building value-added agri-business ecosystems, Muslim nations, states, and cities can increase revenue, generate employment, and strengthen domestic and international trade.

Why Agriculture Matters

1. Revenue Generation

- Export of halal-certified foods and agro-processed goods
- Value-added agricultural industries

2. Food Security

- Reduces dependence on imports
- Strengthens community resilience and stability

3. Employment Creation

- Farming, food processing, logistics, packaging, and retail
- Opportunities across rural and urban areas

4. Cultural and Religious Alignment

- Halal certification ensures trust, quality, and global competitiveness

Case Examples

- **Malaysia** — Integrated palm oil and bioenergy ecosystems generating revenue and employment

- **Turkey** — Modern agri-business hubs exporting high-value crops globally
- **Indonesia** — Global leader in halal-certified food exports and branding

Step 1 — Identify Agricultural Opportunities
Priority Focus Areas

- **Modern Farming:** precision agriculture, hydroponics, greenhouse cultivation
- **Halal Certification:** compliance with international halal standards
- **Agri-Processing:** packaging, canning, frozen and ready-to-eat products
- **Export-Oriented Crops:** high-demand regional and global produce
- **Digital Agri-Markets:** direct farmer-to-buyer platforms

Agri-Business Readiness Checklist

- Soil health and fertility assessment completed
- Irrigation and water efficiency mapped
- Crop selection aligned with market demand
- Cold chain and logistics systems available
- Halal compliance standards implemented

Step 2 — Strategic Approach
Strategy

Develop an **integrated farm-to-market ecosystem** combining production, processing, certification, technology, and export channels.

Farm-to-Factory Integration

- Direct supply chains from farms to processing units
- Reduced intermediaries for higher farmer income
- Consistent quality control for domestic and export markets

Halal Certification & Global Branding

- Obtain internationally recognized halal certifications
- Promote halal identity as a premium global brand
- Partner with global halal compliance bodies

Technology Adoption

- Precision agriculture (drones, sensors, smart irrigation)
- Data-driven crop planning and pest management
- Mobile apps for weather, prices, and training

Market Expansion

- Digital e-market platforms linking farmers to buyers
- Export-focused branding and trade partnerships
- Participation in global food and trade exhibitions

Sustainability Measures

- Organic and climate-smart farming
- Bioenergy and agricultural waste recycling
- Water conservation and soil preservation

Step 3 — State Agri-Development Plan

Purpose

Create a **statewide agricultural transformation roadmap** integrating production, infrastructure, markets, and governance.

Core Components

- **Resource Assessment:** land, water, soil, and climate mapping
- **Infrastructure:** irrigation, cold storage, transport, agro-industrial parks
- **Technology & Training:** digital tools, farmer education, innovation labs
- **Market Integration:** e-markets, exports, halal branding
- **Governance & Compliance:** food safety, certification, subsidy systems

System Blueprint

```
State Agri-Development Plan
├── Resource Assessment
├── Infrastructure & Technology
├── Farmer Training & Support
├── Market Access & Export Promotion
└── Governance & Compliance
```

Step 4 — Business Canvas Application

Block	Details
Value Proposition	High-quality halal agricultural products with domestic and global market reach
Key Activities	Farming, processing, certification, logistics, digital market integration
Key Resources	Land, irrigation systems, processing units, workforce
Key Partners	Farmers, processors, logistics firms, halal certifiers
Revenue Streams	Domestic sales, exports, processed goods, government incentives
Customer Segments	Retailers, wholesalers, global buyers, online consumers
Channels	E-commerce, export networks, retail chains
Customer Relationships	Trust-based, quality assurance, long-term supply contracts
Cost Structure	Inputs, infrastructure, certification, logistics, technology
Metrics	Yield/ha, export volume, revenue growth, compliance rates

Step 5 — Risk Assessment & Mitigation

Risk	Impact	Mitigation
Crop failure	High	Diversification, climate-smart farming, insurance
Market price volatility	Medium	Forward contracts, export agreements
Halal compliance gaps	High	Regular audits and certification training
Logistics bottlenecks	Medium	Cold chain and transport optimization
Water scarcity	Medium	Efficient irrigation and rainwater harvesting

Step 6 — Implementation Timeline

Phase	Activities	Outcome
0–6 Months	Soil analysis, irrigation mapping, farmer engagement	Baseline readiness
6–12 Months	Pilot farms, halal certification, e-market launch	Early adoption and revenue
1–3 Years	Expand processing, training, digital integration	Scaled production and exports
3–5 Years	Global export expansion, advanced agri-tech adoption	Sustainable agri-economy

Step 7 — Community and Cultural Integration

- Engage **local farmers, youth, and women cooperatives**
- Embed **Islamic principles of stewardship (Khilafah)** and ethical farming
- Reinvest agri-profits into **rural development, education, and healthcare**
- Promote community-owned agri-enterprises and cooperatives

Strategic Implementation Mindset

- **Food security first, exports second**
- **Technology-enabled agriculture**
- **Farmer-centric value chains**
- **Halal-certified global competitiveness**
- **Sustainable land and water management**

Conclusion

Agriculture, food security, and agri-business form a **core pillar of long-term economic resilience.**

By:

- Modernizing farming and processing systems
- Integrating halal certification and global trade
- Leveraging technology and sustainable practices
- Building strong farm-to-market value chains

Muslim nations, states, and local communities can achieve **food security, revenue growth, employment generation, and sustainable socio-economic prosperity**.

Chapter 15 — Education and Skill Development as Revenue Engines

Objective

Education and skill development are not only social priorities—they are **strategic economic assets**. By investing in universities, vocational institutes, research ecosystems, and international student programs, Muslim nations, states, and cities can generate sustainable revenue, build human capital, and position themselves as global centers of knowledge, talent, and innovation.

Why Education and Skill Development Matter

1. Revenue Generation

- Tuition fees from domestic and international students
- Research grants and intellectual property commercialization
- Consultancy and executive education programs

2. Employment Creation

- Academic, administrative, and research roles
- Vocational and technical training employment
- Education-linked service industries

3. Human Capital Development

- Skilled workforce aligned with national economic sectors
- Globally employable graduates

4. Innovation and Research

- Development of technology, startups, and patents
- Applied research solving local and global challenges

5. Soft Power and Global Influence

- International student inflow
- Cultural diplomacy through education exchanges

Case Examples

- **Malaysia & UAE** — global education hubs generating revenue through international students
- **Turkey & Indonesia** — vocational training systems supporting industrial sectors
- **Qatar & Saudi Arabia** — research universities attracting global talent and R&D investment

Step 1 — Identify Educational Opportunities
Priority Focus Areas

- **Universities & Higher Education:** international degrees, executive education, online programs
- **Vocational & Technical Institutes:** job-ready, industry-aligned skills
- **International Student Programs:** scholarships, exchange programs, global recruitment
- **Research & Innovation Grants:** applied research tied to industry and national priorities
- **Lifelong Learning:** certification programs, online courses, professional development

Education Readiness Checklist

- Curriculum aligned with local and global market needs
- Faculty recruitment and development programs established
- Enrollment, retention, and graduate tracking systems active

- International partnerships and exchange agreements signed
- Research funding and IP management frameworks in place

Step 2 — Strategic Approach

Strategy

Develop a **globally competitive education ecosystem** that produces talent, drives research, and generates diversified revenue streams.

Scholarships and Funding Programs

- Partial and full scholarships to attract international students
- Research grants aligned with national industries
- PPP-funded vocational training programs

Curriculum and Faculty Excellence

- Regular curriculum audits aligned with global standards
- Continuous faculty training and international exposure
- New programs in AI, fin tech, renewable energy, entrepreneurship

International Collaboration

- Dual-degree and exchange programs
- Joint research initiatives with global universities
- Industry partnerships with multinational companies

Digital Education Ecosystem

- Online degree programs and certifications
- Virtual classrooms and global learning platforms
- Graduate placement platforms linking students to employers

Revenue Diversification

- Tuition (domestic + international)
- Research commercialization and patents
- Consultancy services and executive training

Step 3 — Education Export & Workforce Development Plan

Purpose

Establish a **national and state-level roadmap** to transform education into a major revenue and workforce development engine.

Core Components

- **Market Analysis:** international demand, domestic skill gaps
- **Infrastructure:** campuses, labs, dormitories, digital platforms
- **Faculty & Curriculum:** recruitment, training, global alignment
- **Student Services:** scholarships, orientation, career counseling
- **Governance:** accreditation, quality assurance, compliance

System Blueprint

```
Education Export & Workforce Development Plan
├─ Market Analysis & Demand Mapping
├─ Infrastructure & Technology
├─ Faculty & Curriculum Development
├─ Student Services & International Programs
└─ Governance, Quality & Compliance
```

Step 4 — Business Canvas Application

Block	Details
Value Proposition	Globally competitive, employable workforce and high-quality education
Key Activities	Teaching, training, research, international collaboration
Key Resources	Universities, vocational institutes, faculty, labs, digital platforms
Key Partners	Global universities, industries, governments, research bodies
Revenue Streams	Tuition, research grants, online courses, consultancy
Customer Segments	Students, professionals, industries, governments
Channels	Campus programs, online learning, study-abroad partnerships
Customer Relationships	Mentorship, career services, alumni networks
Cost Structure	Faculty, infrastructure, curriculum, partnerships, marketing
Metrics	Employment rate, student enrollment, research output, revenue growth

Step 5 — Risk Assessment & Mitigation

Risk	Impact	Mitigation
Low enrollment	High	Scholarships, global marketing, partnerships
Curriculum mismatch	Medium	Industry advisory boards, regular reviews
Faculty shortage	Medium	Competitive salaries, international recruitment
Funding gaps	Medium	PPP models, grants, commercialization
Student retention issues	Medium	Mentorship, career counseling, engagement

Step 6 — Implementation Timeline

Phase	Activities	Outcome
0–6 Months	Curriculum audit, faculty mapping, market demand study	Baseline readiness
6–12 Months	Launch scholarships, online platforms, partnerships	Initial enrollment and revenue
1–3 Years	Expand vocational institutes, research centers, international programs	Scaled growth
3–5 Years	Global branding, innovation ecosystems, continuous upgrades	Sustainable education economy

Step 7 — Community and Cultural Integration

- Expand **vocational training access for local communities**
- Embed **Islamic ethics** in business, leadership, and finance education
- Use education revenue for **scholarships and social development**
- Promote **women and youth participation** in higher education and skills training
- Build **community learning hubs** for lifelong education

Strategic Implementation Mindset

- Education as a **revenue sector**, not only a social service
- Skills aligned with **national economic priorities**
- Research tied to **industry and innovation ecosystems**
- Global student attraction as **education exports**
- Lifelong learning as a **continuous revenue stream**

Conclusion

Education and skill development are **transformational economic engines.**

By:

- Building world-class universities and vocational institutes
- Attracting international students and partnerships
- Integrating research, innovation, and industry collaboration
- Leveraging digital learning and lifelong education

Muslim nations, states, and cities can generate **sustainable revenue, high-quality employment, innovation ecosystems, and global influence**, while nurturing a knowledgeable, ethical, and future-ready society.

Chapter 16 — Healthcare as Industry

Objective

Healthcare is not only a fundamental social service but also a powerful economic sector. By strategically investing in **medical tourism, pharmaceuticals, wellness services, and Halal-compliant healthcare systems**, Muslim nations, states, and communities can generate sustainable revenue, create employment, and improve public health outcomes.

This chapter presents a **comprehensive framework** to transform healthcare into a **sustainable, high-impact industry**.

Why Healthcare Matters

Healthcare contributes simultaneously to **economic growth and social well-being**:

- **Revenue Generation**
  Through medical tourism, pharmaceutical exports, wellness services, and allied industries.
- **Employment Creation**
  For doctors, nurses, technicians, researchers, administrators, and support services.
- **Public Health Improvement**
  Healthier populations increase productivity and reduce long-term economic burdens.
- **Global Competitiveness**
  International certifications and Halal-compliant services attract global patients.
- **Innovation & Research**
  Investment in healthcare R&D drives pharmaceuticals, biotechnology, and digital health solutions.

Global Case Examples

- **Malaysia** and **Turkey**
  Established leaders in medical tourism with strong Halal healthcare offerings.
- **Dubai Healthcare City** in **United Arab Emirates**
  An integrated ecosystem combining hospitals, wellness, and medical tourism infrastructure.
- **Indonesia**
  Halal-certified hospitals serving both domestic and international patients.

Step 1 — Identify Healthcare Opportunities
Priority Focus Areas

- **Medical Tourism**
  Specialized care in cardiology, oncology, orthopedics, fertility, and elective procedures.
- **Pharmaceutical Industry**
  Production of Halal-certified medicines, vaccines, and nutraceuticals.
- **Wellness & Preventive Care**
  Fitness, nutrition, rehabilitation, and traditional medicine services.
- **Telemedicine & Digital Health**
  Remote consultations, AI diagnostics, and continuous patient monitoring.
- **Halal Healthcare Compliance**
  Ensuring ethical, dietary, and operational standards aligned with Islamic values.

Healthcare Readiness Checklist

- Accreditation and certification compliance (national + international)
- Skilled workforce recruitment and continuous professional development
- Patient safety and satisfaction systems
- Infrastructure and equipment readiness
- Regulatory and Halal compliance verification

Step 2 — Strategic Development Approach
Core Strategy

Develop a **fully integrated healthcare ecosystem** focused on **quality, compliance, innovation, and global outreach**.

1. Medical Tourism Development

- Halal-compliant hospitals with multilingual staff
- International insurance partnerships
- Structured treatment packages (elective, chronic, emergency care)

2. Pharmaceutical Manufacturing & Export

- Halal-certified medicine and nutraceutical production
- Export to Muslim-majority and global markets
- R&D for innovative therapeutics and preventive healthcare

3. Wellness & Preventive Health

- Fitness, nutrition, and mental health centers
- Integration of **Unani, Ayurveda, and Islamic medicine**
- Corporate and community wellness programs

4. Workforce Development

- Continuous medical education and specialization
- Training in Halal healthcare ethics and patient communication
- Incentives for research and clinical excellence

5. Digital Health Integration

- Telemedicine platforms
- AI-assisted diagnostics and predictive health tools
- Digital records, patient portals, and smart hospital systems

Step 3 — State Healthcare Growth Plan Blueprint

Purpose

To create a **phased, scalable roadmap** for building healthcare as a revenue-generating industry.

Core Components

1. **Infrastructure & Facilities**
   Hospitals, clinics, wellness centers, pharma manufacturing
2. **Talent & Training**
   Recruitment, certification, specialization
3. **International Certification & Halal Compliance**
   ISO, JCI, and Halal standards
4. **Research, Innovation & Digital Health**
   Clinical trials, biotech, AI health systems
5. **Marketing & Medical Tourism Promotion**
   Global outreach, travel partnerships, insurance alliances
6. **Governance & Monitoring**
   Quality assurance, compliance audits, patient feedback

Healthcare Growth Model

State Healthcare Growth Plan
├─ Infrastructure & Facilities

├─ Talent Development & Training
├─ International Certification & Halal Compliance
├─ Research, Innovation & Digital Health
├─ Marketing, Tourism & Patient Acquisition
└─ Governance, Quality Control & Reporting

Step 4 — Business Model Framework

Block	Details
Value Proposition	High-quality, Halal-compliant, globally accredited healthcare
Key Activities	Treatment, wellness programs, pharma production, R&D
Key Resources	Hospitals, equipment, skilled workforce, digital systems
Key Partners	Insurers, travel agencies, universities, pharma distributors
Revenue Streams	Domestic care, medical tourism, pharma exports, wellness, telemedicine
Customer Segments	Citizens, international patients, corporates, governments
Channels	Hospitals, wellness centers, digital platforms, tourism networks
Customer Relationships	Trust-based, patient-centered, culturally aligned
Cost Structure	Infrastructure, salaries, training, equipment, R&D, marketing
Key Metrics	Patient volume, revenue, satisfaction, exports, accreditation

Step 5 — Risk Assessment & Mitigation

Risk	Impact	Mitigation
Regulatory non-compliance	High	Strict adherence to national, international, and Halal standards
Workforce shortages	Medium	Training programs, global recruitment, incentives
Patient safety incidents	High	Clinical governance, emergency protocols, insurance coverage
Cyber security threats	Medium	Secure IT systems, encrypted data, regular audits
Market competition	Medium	Specialization, quality differentiation, Halal positioning

Step 6 — Implementation Timeline

Phase	Key Activities	Outcome
0–6 Months	Infrastructure audit, recruitment, certification	Operational readiness
6–12 Months	Launch tourism packages, wellness programs, telemedicine	Early revenue
1–3 Years	Expand hospitals, pharma production, R&D	Scaled growth
3–5 Years	Full integration, exports, continuous improvement	Sustainable industry

Step 7 — Community & Cultural Integration

- Ensure services are **Halal-compliant and culturally sensitive**
- Promote **preventive healthcare education**
- Use industry revenues to fund:
    - Local clinics
    - Emergency services
    - Rural healthcare access
- Encourage **university–hospital–industry research collaboration**

Conclusion

Healthcare can evolve into a **strategic economic pillar** by:

- Building Halal-compliant hospitals and wellness ecosystems
- Attracting domestic and international patients
- Investing in pharmaceuticals, R&D, and digital health
- Strengthening workforce development and governance

By doing so, Muslim nations, states, and cities can achieve:

✔ Sustainable economic growth

✔ Global healthcare competitiveness

✔ Improved public health outcomes

Healthcare thus becomes a cornerstone of both economic prosperity and social well-being.

Chapter 17 — Public-Private Partnerships (PPP) Blueprint

Objective

Public-Private Partnerships (PPPs) are strategic mechanisms for mobilizing private investment to develop infrastructure, transport, utilities, and social services. They reduce fiscal pressure on governments while improving service quality, accelerating development, and generating sustainable revenue.

This chapter presents a **comprehensive blueprint** for designing, implementing, and governing PPPs as engines of **economic growth, efficiency, and public welfare**.

Why PPPs Matter

PPPs create value across economic, social, and governance dimensions:

- **Revenue Generation**
  Through tolls, service charges, shared investment returns, and long-term concession agreements.
- **Infrastructure Acceleration**
  Faster delivery of roads, rail, ports, hospitals, schools, and digital infrastructure.
- **Risk Sharing**
  Balanced allocation of financial, operational, and regulatory risks between public and private partners.
- **Innovation & Efficiency**
  Private sector expertise in technology, operations, and project management enhances service delivery.
- **Social Impact**
  Improved access to reliable transport, utilities, healthcare, and education.

Global Case Examples

- **Malaysia** and **United Arab Emirates**
  Successful PPPs in highways, airports, and healthcare infrastructure through transparent regulatory systems.
- **Turkey**
  Urban rail and integrated mobility systems funded and operated through PPP agreements.
- **Indonesia**
  Water treatment, housing, and public utilities expanded through PPP-led financing.

Step 1 — Identify PPP Opportunities

Priority Sectors

1. Transport & Mobility

- Highways, metro systems, airports, seaports
- Logistics parks and freight corridors

2. Social Infrastructure

- Hospitals, schools, universities, vocational institutes
- Renewable energy and climate infrastructure

3. Utilities & Essential Services

- Water supply and treatment
- Electricity generation and distribution
- Waste management and broadband connectivity

4. Tourism & Cultural Development

- Heritage site restoration

- Visitor centers and tourism zones
- Entertainment and cultural districts

5. Urban Development

- Smart cities and mixed-use developments
- Commercial complexes and affordable housing

PPP Readiness Checklist

- Completed **feasibility and financial viability studies**
- Cost-benefit and social impact analysis
- Stakeholder mapping and engagement strategy
- Risk identification and allocation framework
- Legal, environmental, and regulatory compliance

Step 2 — Strategic Approach

Core Strategy

Design **transparent, accountable, and mutually beneficial PPP structures** that maximize public value and private returns.

1. Transparent Bidding & Procurement

- Open, competitive tendering
- Clear evaluation criteria (technical + financial)
- Independent auditing and anti-corruption safeguards

2. Revenue-Sharing & Financial Structuring

- Clearly defined investment and concession models
- Performance-linked incentives and penalties
- Long-term sustainability and affordability analysis

3. Risk Management & Oversight

- Identification of financial, operational, environmental, and political risks
- Balanced risk allocation between partners
- Continuous monitoring and third-party audits

4. Citizen-Centric Service Design

- Affordable pricing models
- Universal access and inclusion
- Real-time citizen feedback systems

5. Innovation & Smart Infrastructure

- Digital tolling, smart transport, and IoT-based utilities
- Energy-efficient and climate-resilient infrastructure
- Digital dashboards for project tracking and public transparency

Step 3 — PPP Governance Framework Blueprint

Purpose

To ensure **accountability, transparency, and long-term sustainability** in PPP implementation.

Core Governance Components

1. **Project Identification & Feasibility**
   Market demand, financial viability, and social impact
2. **Legal & Regulatory Framework**
   Contracts, dispute resolution, compliance standards
3. **Partner Selection & Contracting**
   Tendering, evaluation, concession structuring
4. **Performance Monitoring & Reporting**
   KPIs, service standards, financial reporting
5. **Exit & Contingency Planning**

Contract termination, asset transfer, dispute mechanisms

Governance Structure

PPP Governance Framework
├── Project Identification & Feasibility
├── Legal & Regulatory Compliance
├── Partner Selection & Contracting
├── Performance Monitoring & Reporting
└── Exit & Contingency Planning

Step 4 — Business Model Framework

Block	Details
Value Proposition	Efficient, high-quality, sustainable infrastructure and services
Key Activities	Planning, financing, construction, operations, maintenance
Key Resources	Public land/assets, private capital, technical expertise, digital systems
Key Partners	Investors, developers, contractors, operators, regulators
Revenue Streams	Tolls, service charges, concession payments, rentals
Customer Segments	Citizens, commuters, businesses, tourists
Channels	Physical infrastructure, mobile apps, digital platforms
Customer Relationships	Transparent, service-oriented, performance-based
Cost Structure	Capital costs, O&M, financing costs, compliance, monitoring
Key Metrics	ROI, service uptime, cost recovery, satisfaction, compliance

Step 5 — Risk Assessment & Mitigation

Risk	Impact	Mitigation
Cost overruns	High	Fixed-price EPC contracts, contingency reserves
Project delays	High	Milestone-based payments, strict timelines
Regulatory changes	Medium	Strong legal frameworks and policy stability
Revenue shortfall	Medium	Conservative projections, blended revenue streams
Public dissatisfaction	Medium	Feedback systems, grievance redressal

Step 6 — Implementation Timeline

Phase	Activities	Outcome
0–6 Months	Feasibility studies, legal structuring	PPP readiness established
6–12 Months	Tendering, partner selection	Contracts signed
1–3 Years	Construction and rollout	Operational infrastructure
3–5 Years	Optimization and scaling	Sustainable PPP ecosystem

Step 7 — Community & Cultural Integration

- Engage **local communities and SMEs** in project supply chains
- Preserve **cultural heritage and environmental sustainability**
- Ensure **affordable access** to essential services
- Reinvest PPP revenues into:
    - Education
    - Healthcare

    - Community infrastructure

Conclusion

Public-Private Partnerships are powerful instruments for **economic transformation and public service excellence.**

By:

- Selecting high-impact infrastructure projects
- Ensuring transparent governance and bidding
- Structuring performance-based contracts
- Integrating technology, risk management, and citizen participation

Muslim nations, states, and cities can build **world-class infrastructure**, generate **sustainable revenue**, and deliver **high-quality services.**

PPPs thus create a virtuous cycle of growth, efficiency, and inclusive prosperity.

Chapter 18 — Urban Planning for Business Growth

Objective

Urban planning is a powerful engine of **city-level economic growth and prosperity**. When cities are designed with efficient zoning, integrated transportation, mixed-use developments, and smart infrastructure, they become magnets for investment, entrepreneurship, tourism, and high-quality living.

This chapter provides a **comprehensive urban planning framework** to stimulate business growth, increase municipal revenue, and enhance overall livability.

Why Urban Planning Matters

Strategic urban design directly influences economic performance:

- **Revenue Generation**
  Property taxes, business licenses, tourism income, and commercial rental streams
- **Business Expansion**
  Dedicated commercial zones, tech hubs, industrial parks, and innovation districts
- **Efficiency & Sustainability**
  Smart mobility systems, energy-efficient infrastructure, and green spaces
- **Social Harmony & Livability**
  Balanced integration of residential, commercial, and recreational areas
- **Investment Attraction**
  Well-planned cities draw both domestic and international investors

Global Case Examples

- **Dubai**
  Mixed-use development, free zones, and integrated transport networks attracting global investment.
- **Istanbul**
  Harmonious blend of historic preservation with modern business districts and tourism zones.
- **Kuala Lumpur**
  Transit-oriented development and smart zoning driving urban economic growth.

Step 1 — Identify Planning Opportunities
Key Focus Areas
1. Zoning Optimization

- Clear designation of industrial, commercial, residential, and mixed-use zones
- Prevention of land-use conflicts and congestion

2. Transport Integration

- Roads, metro, rail, bus rapid transit (BRT)
- Pedestrian walkways and cycling infrastructure
- Freight and logistics corridors

3. Commercial Clusters

- Central business districts (CBDs)
- Technology parks and innovation hubs
- Retail and wholesale marketplaces

4. Public Spaces & Tourism Zones

- Parks, waterfronts, plazas
- Cultural and historical districts
- Event venues and entertainment hubs

5. Smart City Systems

- IoT sensors and traffic analytics
- Real-time urban dashboards
- Digital citizen service platforms

Urban Planning Readiness Checklist

- Land-use and cadastral mapping completed
- Traffic flow and transport coverage analysis
- Public space availability and utilization assessment
- Environmental and energy impact evaluation
- Commercial and industrial zone performance review

Step 2 — Strategic Approach

Core Strategy

Design **integrated, investor-friendly, and livable urban environments** that foster commerce, innovation, and community well-being.

1. Incentivize Commercial Clusters

- Tax incentives for startups and SMEs in business zones
- Reliable utilities: electricity, broadband, water
- Co-located incubators and innovation centers

2. Smart Mobility Integration

- Public transit connecting residential, commercial, and industrial zones

- Multi-modal transport systems (metro + buses + cycling)
- AI-driven traffic and logistics management

3. Streamlined Regulatory Systems

- Digital single-window permit and licensing systems
- Online inspections and compliance platforms
- Regular zoning and regulatory updates aligned with economic priorities

4. Mixed-Use Development

- Residential units integrated with retail and office space
- Walkable neighborhoods with co-working and leisure areas
- Efficient land use and higher economic productivity per square kilometer

5. Sustainability & Urban Resilience

- Green building standards and renewable energy integration
- Water conservation, waste recycling, and urban forests
- Climate-resilient and disaster-resistant infrastructure

Step 3 — City Master Plan Blueprint

Purpose

Provide a **visual and operational roadmap** for sustainable urban economic growth.

Core Components

1. **Zoning Map**
   Industrial, commercial, residential, mixed-use, and leisure zones
2. **Transport & Mobility Network**

Road, rail, metro, BRT, pedestrian, and cycling systems

3. **Economic Clusters**
   CBDs, tech parks, SME hubs, tourism districts
4. **Public Infrastructure**
   Parks, cultural facilities, utilities, energy, water
5. **Regulatory Dashboard**
   Permits, incentives, compliance, urban performance monitoring

Master Plan Structure

City Master Plan
├─ Zoning Optimization
├─ Transport & Mobility Integration
├─ Economic Clusters Development
├─ Public Spaces & Tourism Infrastructure
└─ Regulatory & Governance Dashboard

Step 4 — Urban Business Model Framework

Block	Details
Value Proposition	Livable, efficient, investor-friendly city with strong business ecosystems
Key Activities	Urban design, infrastructure development, regulatory facilitation
Key Resources	Land, municipal governance, transport systems, digital platforms
Key Partners	Developers, investors, planners, transport authorities, SMEs
Revenue Streams	Property taxes, business permits, tourism, parking, leasing
Customer Segments	Residents, investors, entrepreneurs, tourists
Channels	City portals, business hubs, digital apps
Customer Relationships	Transparent, participatory, service-oriented
Cost Structure	Infrastructure CAPEX, maintenance, enforcement, technology
Metrics	Business occupancy, tax revenue, congestion reduction, citizen satisfaction

Step 5 — Risk Assessment & Mitigation

Risk	Impact	Mitigation
Land-use conflicts	High	Zoning enforcement and stakeholder consultation
Traffic congestion	Medium	Smart mobility and public transport expansion
Investment shortfalls	Medium	PPPs, tax incentives, investor outreach
Regulatory delays	Medium	Digital approval systems and policy reform
Environmental stress	Medium	Green codes, renewable energy, urban parks

Step 6 — Implementation Timeline

Phase	Activities	Outcome
0–6 Months	Land-use audits, zoning review, traffic studies	Baseline planning
6–12 Months	Smart mobility design, cluster identification	Pilot zones launched
1–3 Years	Mixed-use construction, infrastructure upgrades	Active business districts
3–5 Years	Full integration of transport, tourism, and clusters	Mature urban economy

Step 7 — Community & Cultural Integration

- Encourage **citizen participation** in planning decisions
- Integrate **heritage and cultural landmarks** into commercial districts
- Ensure **equitable access** to transport, parks, and services
- Reinvest urban revenues into:
    - Education
    - Healthcare
    - Community development

Conclusion

Urban planning is a **cornerstone of city prosperity and economic resilience.**

By:

- Optimizing zoning and transport networks
- Building mixed-use and commercial clusters
- Streamlining regulatory systems
- Integrating sustainability and smart technology

Cities can:

- Attract investment
- Generate strong municipal revenues
- Improve quality of life
- Foster long-term economic growth

Well-planned cities become engines of innovation, commerce, and social well-being—creating thriving, self-sustaining urban economies.

Chapter 19 — Creative Economy and Cultural Industries

Objective

The **creative economy**—spanning film, music, visual arts, design, heritage, and digital media—represents a powerful and scalable engine for **economic growth, cultural preservation, and global influence.**

For Muslim nations, states, cities, and neighborhoods, investing in cultural industries enables:

- Sustainable revenue generation
- Job creation and entrepreneurship
- Preservation of Islamic and local heritage
- International cultural visibility and soft power

This chapter presents a **strategic framework for building a vibrant, revenue-generating creative ecosystem.**

Why the Creative Economy Matters

A well-developed creative sector contributes across multiple economic and social dimensions:

Revenue Generation

Ticket sales, licensing, royalties, streaming, merchandising, exhibitions, and intellectual property monetization

Employment & Entrepreneurship

Jobs for artists, filmmakers, musicians, designers, writers, producers, event managers, and digital creators

Cultural Preservation

Safeguarding and promoting Islamic art, architecture, crafts, literature, and traditions

Tourism Development

Cultural districts, festivals, galleries, and film locations attracting global visitors

Global Reach

Digital platforms enable local cultural content to reach international markets

Global Case Examples

- **Istanbul** and **Cairo**
  Film festivals, cultural districts, and music industries driving tourism and creative exports
- **Malaysia** and **United Arab Emirates**
  Creative incubators, design parks, and media zones boosting creative sector GDP
- **Indonesia** and **Morocco**
  Handicrafts, textiles, and traditional arts integrated with global e-commerce markets

Step 1 — Identify Creative Economy Opportunities

Core Focus Areas

1. Film & Media

- Film studios and post-production facilities
- Animation and visual effects
- Streaming and digital distribution platforms

2. Music & Performing Arts

- Recording studios and live venues
- Orchestras, theatre groups, and cultural performances
- Regional and international music festivals

3. Visual Arts & Crafts

- Galleries and exhibition spaces
- Artisan workshops and craft hubs

- Export of traditional handicrafts and Islamic art

4. Digital Media & Gaming

- App development and game studios
- Content creation (video, podcasts, design)
- Online creative marketplaces

5. Cultural Tourism

- Heritage districts and museums
- Film tourism and creative tours
- Interactive and immersive cultural experiences

Creative Economy Readiness Checklist

- Talent registry and skill mapping completed
- Annual cultural calendar and event pipeline defined
- Infrastructure audit (studios, galleries, theaters, co-working spaces)
- Funding and grant mechanisms established
- Digital platforms for marketing, streaming, and e-commerce operational

Step 2 — Strategic Approach

Core Strategy

Develop a **sustainable, inclusive, and globally competitive creative ecosystem** connecting creators, markets, investors, and audiences.

1. Talent Development & Incubation

- Scholarships, grants, and artist residencies
- Creative incubators and shared workspaces

- Partnerships with universities and international cultural institutions

2. Infrastructure & Cultural Districts

- Dedicated creative zones with:
  - Studios
  - Galleries
  - Theaters
  - Co-working spaces
- Integrated cafés, retail, and public spaces to increase visitor engagement

3. Events & Festival Strategy

- Annual:
  - Film festivals
  - Music festivals
  - Art biennales
- Workshops, exhibitions, master classes
- Global promotion through media and streaming platforms

4. Digital & Global Integration

- E-commerce for crafts and art exports
- Streaming platforms for film, music, and performances
- Social media marketing targeting global audiences

5. Cultural Preservation & Branding

- Promote Islamic heritage through creative storytelling
- Collaborate with historians, architects, and scholars
- Position cities and districts as **global cultural destinations**

Step 3 — Cultural Economy Development Blueprint

Purpose

Provide a structured roadmap for implementing **city and neighborhood-level creative economy ecosystems**

Core Components

1. **Talent & Skill Mapping**
   Registry of artists, creators, technicians
2. **Infrastructure Planning**
   Studios, galleries, theaters, creative labs
3. **Event Programming**
   Festivals, exhibitions, competitions, workshops
4. **Funding & Investment**
   Government grants, private investors, cultural foundations
5. **Digital Platforms**
   E-commerce, streaming, e-learning
6. **Monitoring & Metrics**
   Revenue, audience engagement, participation, exports

Development Framework

Cultural Economy Development Plan
├─ Talent Development & Incubation
├─ Infrastructure & Creative Districts
├─ Festivals & Event Programming
├─ Funding, Grants & Investments
├─ Digital & Global Integration
└─ Performance Monitoring & Metrics

Step 4 — Creative Economy Business Model

Block	Details
Value Proposition	Monetized cultural heritage combined with modern creative innovation
Key Activities	Content production, exhibitions, events, workshops, digital publishing
Key Resources	Talent, cultural venues, digital platforms, funding mechanisms
Key Partners	Artists, NGOs, cultural institutions, universities, investors
Revenue Streams	Ticket sales, royalties, e-commerce, sponsorships, grants
Customer Segments	Tourists, local audiences, collectors, digital consumers
Channels	Festivals, galleries, online platforms, social media
Customer Relationships	Participatory, community-driven, collaborative
Cost Structure	Talent support, infrastructure, event production, marketing
Metrics	Attendance, revenue, exports, artist participation, global reach

Step 5 — Risk Assessment & Mitigation

Risk	Impact	Mitigation
Talent migration	Medium	Grants, recognition programs, career pathways
Funding shortages	High	Public-private funding, sponsorships, crowd funding
Cultural misalignment	Medium	Community consultation and advisory boards
Market saturation	Medium	Niche branding and international positioning
Infrastructure underuse	Medium	Multi-purpose venues and co-working integration

Step 6 — Implementation Timeline

Phase	Activities	Outcome
0–6 Months	Talent registry, audits, funding setup	Foundation established
6–12 Months	Incubators, pilot exhibitions, small events	Early engagement and revenue
1–3 Years	Festivals, creative districts, digital platforms	Scaled growth and tourism
3–5 Years	Global branding, exports, partnerships	Sustainable creative economy

Step 7 — Community & Cultural Integration

- Ensure **inclusive participation** across communities and youth
- Preserve Islamic heritage alongside modern creative expression
- Encourage **community engagement through festivals and workshops**
- Reinvest creative economy revenue into:
    - Education

- Social development
- Cultural infrastructure

Conclusion

The creative economy is a **strategic pillar of modern prosperity.** By:

- Developing creative districts and incubators
- Supporting artists with funding and infrastructure
- Leveraging digital platforms for global reach
- Integrating culture with tourism and community engagement

Muslim cities and neighborhoods can:

- Generate sustainable revenue
- Strengthen cultural identity
- Create employment and entrepreneurship
- Achieve global cultural recognition

When culture is empowered, economies grow—and communities thrive.

Chapter 20 — Smart City Infrastructure

Objective

Smart city infrastructure leverages IoT, AI, and data analytics to optimize public utilities, services, and safety, while creating new revenue streams and economic efficiency. This chapter outlines a strategic framework to implement a fully integrated smart city ecosystem.

Why Smart City Infrastructure Matters

Efficiency Gains: Reduced energy consumption, optimized traffic flow, and better waste management.

Revenue Generation: Savings in operational costs, monetization of data-driven services, and public-private innovation programs.

Public Safety: Real-time monitoring of crime, accidents, and environmental hazards.

Citizen Engagement: Digital platforms for service requests, grievance redressal, and participatory planning.

Investment Attraction: Cities with advanced technology ecosystems attract businesses, startups, and tech talent.

Case Examples

- **Singapore**: Sensor-driven traffic management and energy optimization saving millions in municipal costs.
- **Dubai**: AI-enabled government services and public safety dashboards.
- **Istanbul** & **Kuala Lumpur**: Smart street lighting, public Wi-Fi, and integrated emergency response systems.

Step 1 — Identify Smart Infrastructure Opportunities

Focus Areas

- **Utilities:** Water, electricity, gas, and waste management systems

- **Public Transport & Mobility:** IoT-enabled traffic signals, smart parking, predictive public transport scheduling
- **Public Safety & Security:** AI-based surveillance, emergency alert systems, disaster monitoring
- **Healthcare & Social Services:** Telemedicine platforms, emergency response coordination
- **Citizen Engagement Platforms:** E-governance portals, feedback apps, digital payment systems

Checklist — Smart City Readiness Assessment

- Existing digital infrastructure audit (connectivity, sensors, data collection)
- City service KPIs and performance metrics
- Security and data privacy protocols assessment
- Stakeholder mapping: government, private partners, technology providers
- Budget and funding sources for IoT deployment

Step 2 — Strategic Approach

Strategy

Build a **data-driven, citizen-centric, and economically sustainable smart city ecosystem.**

Core Components

1. Sensor & IoT Network Deployment

- Smart meters for electricity, water, and gas
- Environmental sensors for air quality, temperature, noise, and pollution
- Traffic monitoring and smart street lighting

2. Integrated Data Dashboards

- Real-time monitoring of city services
- Predictive analytics for resource allocation and emergency response
- Centralized decision-making for city planners

3. AI-Driven Service Optimization

- Predictive maintenance for utilities and public transport
- AI-based resource allocation for hospitals, schools, and emergency services
- Dynamic traffic and crowd management

4. Public-Private Collaboration

- Joint innovation programs with tech companies
- Data-sharing agreements for urban analytics
- Incentives for startups and SMEs

5. Security & Privacy Management

- Cyber security frameworks for IoT systems
- Data privacy policies aligned with national standards
- Public awareness campaigns on responsible data use

Step 3 — Smart City Operations Blueprint

Purpose

Provide a structured roadmap to implement, operate, and scale smart city initiatives.

Components

- **Infrastructure Deployment Plan:** IoT sensors, communication networks, control centers
- **Integrated Operations Center:** Central dashboard

monitoring all city services

- **Data Management & Analytics:** Predictive algorithms and AI insights
- **Public Engagement Platforms:** Citizen apps, digital services, feedback systems
- **Partnership & Innovation Programs:** Collaboration with tech firms and universities
- **Performance & KPI Tracking:** Efficiency, uptime, satisfaction, cost savings

Visual Concept

```
Integrated Smart City Operations
├── IoT & Sensor Deployment
├── Data Collection & Analytics
├── AI Service Optimization
├── Public Engagement Platforms
├── Public-Private Partnerships
└── Performance Monitoring & Reporting
```

Step 4 — Business Canvas Application

Block	Details
Value Proposition	Optimized, efficient, and secure city services
Key Activities	IoT deployment, AI analytics, monitoring, emergency management
Key Resources	Technology platforms, sensors, data centers, skilled workforce
Key Partners	Tech providers, startups, utilities, government agencies
Revenue Streams	Cost savings, service fees, data monetization, innovation programs
Customer Segments	Citizens, businesses, government agencies, tourists
Channels	Mobile apps, dashboards, kiosks, digital portals
Customer Relationships	Transparent, real-time, participatory
Cost Structure	Infrastructure, IT systems, maintenance, analytics
Metrics	Energy savings, response times, uptime, engagement, ROI

Step 5 — Risk Assessment & Mitigation

Risk	Impact	Mitigation
Cyber security breaches	High	Encryption, firewalls, audits, staff training
Technology obsolescence	Medium	Modular upgrades, vendor contracts
Public resistance	Medium	Awareness campaigns, participatory planning
Budget overruns	Medium	Phased deployment, PPP funding
Infrastructure downtime	Medium	Redundancy systems, predictive maintenance

Step 6 — Implementation Timeline

Phase	Activities	Outcome
Phase 1 (**0–6 months**)	Connectivity audit, sensor mapping, Cyber security framework	Baseline readiness
Phase 2 (6–12 months)	IoT deployment, dashboards, pilot AI programs	Operational monitoring
Phase 3 (**1–3 years**)	City-wide integration, citizen apps rollout	Efficient smart services
Phase 4 (**3–5 years**)	Advanced analytics, innovation labs	Fully integrated smart city

Step 7 — Community and Cultural Integration

- Engage residents via citizen dashboards and participatory apps
- Use data insights to enhance tourism, events, and cultural programs
- Ensure equitable access to digital services across all neighborhoods
- Reinvest savings into education, healthcare, and social programs

Conclusion

Smart city infrastructure is not merely a technological upgrade—it is a **complete economic, social, and governance transformation**.

By:

- Deploying IoT and AI for efficiency and safety
- Integrating citizen engagement platforms
- Leveraging public-private innovation partnerships
- Monitoring performance and optimizing services

Cities can **maximize revenue, improve quality of life, attract investment, and build resilient, future-ready urban ecosystems**—creating thriving, sustainable Muslim communities for the future.

Chapter 21 — Local Marketplaces and Entrepreneurship Ecosystems

Objective

Neighborhoods and cities thrive when entrepreneurial ecosystems are nurtured. By fostering startups, SMEs, and co-working environments, communities can generate revenue, create jobs, and stimulate innovation. This chapter outlines a strategic framework for establishing a comprehensive entrepreneurship ecosystem.

Why Local Marketplaces & Entrepreneurship Matter

Revenue Generation: Business registration fees, taxation, commercial leases, and local services

Job Creation: SMEs and startups are major employment drivers, especially for youth and women

Innovation & Competitiveness: Local innovation hubs accelerate technology adoption and new business models

Community Engagement: Markets and co-working spaces strengthen social networks and civic life

Investor Attraction: Structured ecosystems attract private capital and global partnerships

Case Examples

- **Istanbul** & **Dubai**: Co-working districts and startup accelerators supporting SMEs
- **Kuala Lumpur**: Government-backed seed funds and SME mentorship programs
- **Jakarta**: Community marketplaces integrated with digital payment ecosystems for micro-business growth

Step 1 — Identify Entrepreneurial Opportunities

Focus Areas

- **Startup Hubs:** Technology, fin tech, digital content, halal product innovation
- **SME Incubators:** Manufacturing, services, handicrafts, local commerce
- **Co-Working Spaces:** Shared offices enabling networking and collaboration
- **Local Marketplaces:** Neighborhood bazaars, trade fairs, digital marketplaces
- **Investment Networks:** Angel investors, venture capital, microfinance

Checklist — Ecosystem Readiness Assessment

- Mapping of SME density and startup activity
- Availability and capacity of co-working infrastructure
- Ease of business registration and legal support
- Funding pipeline mapping (public and private)
- Mentorship networks and training programs

Step 2 — Strategic Approach

Strategy

Create a **dynamic, inclusive, and revenue-generating entrepreneurial ecosystem** where startups, SMEs, and community markets interconnect and scale together.

Core Pillars

1. Mentorship & Skill Development

- Pair entrepreneurs with mentors from industry and academia
- Workshops on business planning, finance, marketing, and digital skills
- Incubation programs aligned with halal and culturally appropriate business models

2. Seed Funding & Investment Facilitation

- Public-private seed funds and grants
- Microfinance for local and home-based enterprises
- Investor networking events and pitch platforms

3. Infrastructure Development

- Co-working spaces, startup hubs, maker labs
- High-speed internet, meeting rooms, prototyping tools
- Logistics integration for product distribution

4. Local Market Development

- Weekly or monthly community marketplaces
- Digital platforms for micro-business sales
- Branding and promotion of culturally rooted products

5. Policy & Regulatory Support

- Simplified business registration and licensing
- Tax incentives and subsidies for SMEs
- Streamlined intellectual property and compliance processes

Step 3 — City Entrepreneurship Growth Map Blueprint

Purpose

Provide a structured roadmap for developing a city-wide entrepreneurial ecosystem.

Components

- **Startup & SME Mapping:** Identify high-growth sectors and neighborhoods
- **Infrastructure Allocation:** Co-working hubs, innovation

centers, marketplace zones

- **Funding & Mentorship Networks:** Grants, investors, mentor matching systems
- **Events & Market Calendar:** Trade fairs, expos, workshops, networking sessions
- **Digital Integration:** Online marketplaces, e-learning platforms, promotion tools
- **Monitoring & Metrics:** Business growth, job creation, investment inflows

Visual Concept

City Entrepreneurship Growth Map
├─ Startup Hubs
├─ SME Incubators
├─ Co-Working Spaces
├─ Neighborhood Marketplaces
├─ Funding & Mentorship Network
└─ Digital Integration & Monitoring

Step 4 — Business Canvas Application

Block	Details
Value Proposition	Incubation, training, and scaling support for startups and SMEs
Key Activities	Mentorship, training, funding facilitation, co-working management
Key Resources	Workspaces, mentors, digital tools, funding pools
Key Partners	Entrepreneurs, investors, universities, NGOs, local authorities
Revenue Streams	Registration fees, rentals, events, public subsidies
Customer Segments	Startups, SMEs, investors, community entrepreneurs
Channels	Incubators, digital platforms, marketplaces, trade fairs
Customer Relationships	Collaborative, mentorship-driven, transparent
Cost Structure	Infrastructure, programs, events, digital platforms
Metrics	Startups launched, jobs created, revenue growth, investments

Step 5 — Risk Assessment & Mitigation

Risk	Impact	Mitigation
Entrepreneurial failure	Medium	Mentorship, diversified funding, skills training
Funding gaps	High	Blend public, private, and community capital
Market saturation	Medium	Focus on niche and culturally aligned products
Infrastructure underuse	Medium	Multi-purpose hubs, flexible workspaces
Regulatory barriers	Medium	Simplified compliance and advisory services

Step 6 — Implementation Timeline

Phase	**Activities**	**Outcome**
Phase 1 (0–6 months)	Map entrepreneurs, assess infrastructure, formalize businesses	Ecosystem baseline
Phase 2 (6–12 months)	Launch incubators, mentorship programs, local markets	Early-stage revenue and jobs
Phase 3 (1–3 years)	Expand co-working, digital marketplaces, funding programs	Scaled ecosystem
Phase 4 (3–5 years)	Integrate global investors, export products, expand hubs	Sustainable economic growth

Step 7 — Community and Cultural Integration

- Encourage businesses aligned with Islamic values and local cultural identity
- Promote youth and women participation in entrepreneurship
- Use marketplace revenues to support education, healthcare, and community programs
- Integrate local markets into tourism and creative economy sectors

Conclusion

Local marketplaces and entrepreneurship ecosystems are **powerful engines of economic resilience and social empowerment**.

By:

- Establishing startup hubs, SME incubators, and co-working infrastructure
- Providing mentorship, seed funding, and investment access
- Developing vibrant physical and digital marketplaces
- Supporting entrepreneurs through policy and community engagement

Cities can **generate revenue, create employment, preserve cultural identity, and attract investment**—building **self-sustaining, innovative, and prosperous Muslim communities** for the future.

Chapter 22 — Civic Branding and City Marketing

Objective

Civic branding transforms a city into a magnet for investment, talent, and tourism. By creating a strong, cohesive identity, cities can attract economic opportunities, foster cultural pride, and stimulate social cohesion. This chapter outlines a strategic framework for city promotion and branding.

Why Civic Branding Matters

Investment Attraction: Investors favor cities with a clear identity, vision, and credibility

Talent Retention & Recruitment: Skilled professionals choose cities with opportunity, culture, and quality of life

Tourism Boost: Strong branding highlights heritage, culture, and unique experiences

Civic Pride & Engagement: Residents feel connected to a recognizable, respected city identity

Revenue Generation: Increased business activity, tourism income, and sponsorship opportunities

Case Examples

- **Istanbul**: "City of History and Innovation" positioning attracts tourism and international events
- **Dubai**: Global expos and investment forums boost international visibility
- **Kuala Lumpur** & **Lahore**: Festivals and cultural campaigns linking identity with economic growth

Step 1 — Identify Branding Opportunities

Focus Areas

- **City Identity:** Heritage, Islamic significance, culture, and innovation
- **Flagship Projects & Landmarks:** Iconic architecture, heritage districts, waterfronts, and cultural hubs
- **Events & Conferences:** Trade fairs, global summits, festivals, and exhibitions
- **Digital Presence:** Websites, apps, virtual tours, and storytelling platforms
- **Media & PR:** National and international campaigns showcasing achievements

Checklist — Civic Branding Readiness

- Brand audit: current perception, logos, messaging
- Stakeholder alignment: government, business, and cultural sectors
- Identification of unique differentiators
- Marketing calendar with events and campaigns
- Investor and tourism engagement strategies

Step 2 — Strategic Approach

Strategy

Create a **cohesive, credible, and globally visible city brand** aligned with economic growth and cultural identity.

Core Pillars

1. City Brand Creation

- Develop tagline, logo, and messaging framework
- Highlight heritage, Islamic culture, and innovation
- Integrate brand identity across all city communications

2. Events & Conferences

- Host global expos, trade fairs, and cultural festivals
- Promote Islamic arts, heritage, and Halal industries
- Partner with international organizations and media

3. Digital Marketing & Social Media

- Launch city websites, apps, and global campaigns
- Offer virtual tours, interactive maps, and storytelling
- Collaborate with influencers and digital creators

4. Investor Relations & Promotion

- Organize investor summits and networking events
- Provide incentives for startups, SMEs, and large investors
- Maintain transparent economic data and city plans

5. Tourism Marketing

- Promote heritage districts, mosques, cultural centers, and festivals
- Collaborate with airlines, travel agencies, and hotels
- Develop experiential tourism narratives and packages

Step 3 — City Promotion & Investment Strategy Blueprint

Purpose

Provide a structured roadmap for civic branding and economic promotion.

Components

- **Brand Identity Development:** Logo, slogan, messaging, digital design
- **Stakeholder Alignment:** Government, private sector, cultural institutions

- **Events Calendar:** Festivals, expos, conferences, exhibitions
- **Digital & Media Strategy:** Social media, content marketing, PR campaigns
- **Investor Relations Framework:** Summits, investment guides, incentives
- **Monitoring & KPIs:** Brand reach, tourism growth, investment inflows

Visual Concept

City Promotion & Investment Strategy
├── Brand Identity Development
├── Stakeholder Alignment
├── Events & Festivals
├── Digital & Media Campaigns
├── Investor Relations Programs
└── Performance Monitoring & KPIs

Step 4 — Business Canvas Application

Block	Details
Value Proposition	A globally recognized city brand attracting investment, talent, and tourism
Key Activities	Branding, events, marketing, investor engagement, tourism promotion
Key Resources	Marketing teams, digital platforms, cultural assets, venues
Key Partners	Businesses, cultural institutions, media agencies, investors
Revenue Streams	Tourism spending, event fees, sponsorships, investment inflows
Customer Segments	Investors, tourists, residents, skilled professionals
Channels	Social media, websites, expos, conferences, PR campaigns
Customer Relationships	Transparent, participatory, trust-driven
Cost Structure	Marketing, events, digital content, staffing
Metrics	Tourist arrivals, investment deals, social reach, brand recognition

Step 5 — Risk Assessment & Mitigation

Risk	Impact	Mitigation
Weak brand perception	High	Brand audits, global PR campaigns, consistent messaging
Low citizen participation	Medium	Community engagement and cultural involvement
Event failures	Medium	Risk planning, sponsorship management, logistics backups
Budget constraints	Medium	Public-private partnerships and phased campaigns
Competitive positioning	Medium	Focus on unique cultural and economic strengths

Step 6 — Implementation Timeline

Phase	Activities	Outcome
Phase 1 (0–6 months)	Brand audit, stakeholder consultations, messaging design	Brand baseline
Phase 2 (6–12 months)	Launch digital platforms, cultural festivals, PR campaigns	Early visibility
Phase 3 (1–3 years)	Host global conferences, tourism drives, investor summits	Investment & tourism growth
Phase 4 (3–5 years)	Establish global brand recognition and sustain campaigns	Long-term economic impact

Step 7 — Community and Cultural Integration

- Engage residents, artists, and youth in branding campaigns
- Promote Halal tourism and culturally rooted entrepreneurship
- Integrate branding with creative industries and marketplaces
- Reinvest tourism and investment revenue into public services and cultural preservation

Conclusion

Civic branding and city marketing are **powerful economic and cultural strategies**.

By:

- Crafting a clear and culturally aligned city identity
- Hosting international events and festivals
- Leveraging digital marketing for global reach
- Building strong investor relations and tourism promotion

Cities can **attract capital, talent, and visitors**, turning identity into revenue while fostering pride, unity, and long-term prosperity for Muslim communities.

Chapter 23 — Micro-Entrepreneurship and Community Cooperatives

Objective

Neighborhoods thrive when micro-businesses and cooperatives provide local employment, goods, and services. By fostering small-scale production, shared resources, and community-led enterprises, neighborhoods can generate revenue, strengthen social bonds, and build resilient local economies.

Why Micro-Entrepreneurship & Cooperatives Matter

Local Revenue Generation: Money circulates within the neighborhood, boosting economic activity

Job Creation: Small enterprises create employment for youth, women, and marginalized groups

Community Cohesion: Cooperatives foster shared ownership, trust, and responsibility

Skills Development: Entrepreneurs gain practical production, financial, and management skills

Economic Resilience: Diverse local businesses reduce dependency on external supply chains

Case Examples

- Moroccan and Turkish bazaars: Cooperative handicrafts and food products exported globally
- Kashmir & Indonesia: Micro-produce cooperatives supplying local markets and e-commerce
- **Jakarta**: Urban co-working and maker spaces supporting neighborhood entrepreneurship

Step 1 — Identify Neighborhood Opportunities

Focus Areas

- **Micro-Businesses:** Tailoring, food services, repair shops, handicrafts, local digital services
- **Community Cooperatives:** Shared production, credit unions, marketing co-ops
- **Skill-Based Workshops:** Training in crafts, halal production, and digital services
- **Local E-Commerce Platforms:** Online marketplaces for neighborhood goods
- **Neighborhood Services:** Childcare, transport, delivery, maintenance services

Checklist — Neighborhood Ecosystem Assessment

- Mapping of existing businesses and growth potential
- Evaluation of local skills and production capabilities
- Microfinance and funding availability
- Cooperative charters and governance structures drafted
- Digital readiness for marketing and e-commerce

Step 2 — Strategic Approach

Strategy

Create a **self-sustaining neighborhood entrepreneurship ecosystem** supported by training, finance, cooperative structures, and market access.

Core Pillars

1. Skill Training & Capacity Building

- Workshops in production, marketing, finance, and e-commerce
- Mentorship from experienced entrepreneurs and industry experts
- Certification for quality, halal compliance, and licensing

2. Microfinance & Funding Support

- Small loans, grants, and revolving funds for entrepreneurs
- Cooperative pooling for shared equipment and infrastructure
- Partnerships with banks, NGOs, and municipal programs

3. Cooperative Formation & Support

- Legal registration and governance charters
- Democratic decision-making and profit-sharing structures
- Shared facilities such as kitchens, workshops, storage, and retail

4. Market Access & E-Commerce

- Weekly bazaars, pop-up markets, and retail stalls
- Digital platforms for online sales and promotion
- Integration with city logistics, tourism, and cultural markets

5. Policy & Regulatory Facilitation

- Simplified business registration processes
- Tax incentives or exemptions for cooperatives
- Support for halal and culturally aligned production

Step 3 — Neighborhood Entrepreneurship Hub Blueprint

Purpose

Create a centralized hub for training, production, marketing, and cooperative management.

Components

- **Production Units:** Shared kitchens, workshops, craft facilities

- **Skill Development Center:** Training rooms, digital labs, mentorship areas
- **Market & Retail Spaces:** Local bazaars, small shops, pop-up stalls
- **E-Commerce Desk:** Digital marketing, product photography, online sales
- **Microfinance Office:** Loans, savings programs, cooperative funds
- **Community Engagement Center:** Meetings, workshops, governance forums

Visual Concept

```
Neighborhood Entrepreneurship Hub
├── Production Units
├── Skill Development & Mentorship
├── Market & Retail Spaces
├── E-Commerce Support
├── Microfinance & Funding
└── Community Engagement & Governance
```

Step 4 — Business Canvas Application

Block	Details
Value Proposition	Empower neighborhood entrepreneurs and cooperatives to generate sustainable income
Key Activities	Production, training, marketing, e-commerce, cooperative management
Key Resources	Shared facilities, trainers, digital tools, cooperative funds
Key Partners	Entrepreneurs, NGOs, banks, local authorities, community leaders
Revenue Streams	Local sales, online transactions, cooperative profits, service fees
Customer Segments	Residents, local markets, regional buyers, online consumers
Channels	Bazaars, retail stalls, digital platforms, city supply chains
Customer Relationships	Community-based, trust-driven, mentorship-oriented
Cost Structure	Infrastructure, salaries, equipment, marketing, maintenance
Metrics	Businesses created, jobs generated, revenue growth, cooperative participation

Step 5 — Risk Assessment & Mitigation

Risk	Impact	Mitigation
Business failure	Medium	Mentorship, training, phased funding, cooperative risk-sharing
Limited market access	High	E-commerce, distribution partnerships, tourism integration
Funding shortages	Medium	Revolving funds, grants, municipal support
Governance challenges	Medium	Clear cooperative charters and accountability systems
Product quality inconsistency	Medium	Certification, training, and quality audits

Step 6 — Implementation Timeline

Phase	Activities	Outcome
Phase 1 (0–6 months)	Map businesses, identify cooperatives, design hub	Baseline readiness
Phase 2 (6–12 months)	Launch training, establish production units, register cooperatives	Early revenue and participation
Phase 3 (1–3 years)	Expand markets, integrate e-commerce, grow membership	Sustainable local economy
Phase 4 (3–5 years)	Integrate with city supply chains and tourism networks	Self-sufficient ecosystem

Step 7 — Community and Cultural Integration

- Promote locally produced goods aligned with Islamic and cultural values
- Encourage youth, women, and marginalized groups to participate
- Use cooperative revenues to support schools, healthcare, and social programs
- Link neighborhood markets to city-level tourism and

branding initiatives

Conclusion

Micro-entrepreneurship and community cooperatives are **powerful engines of grassroots economic development.**

By:

- Establishing shared production and training hubs
- Supporting entrepreneurs through mentorship and microfinance
- Connecting businesses to local and digital markets
- Integrating cultural and halal production practices

Neighborhoods can generate sustainable income, strengthen social cohesion, and contribute meaningfully to the broader city economy—building **resilient, self-reliant, and prosperous Muslim communities.**

Chapter 24 — Halal Certification and Niche Markets

Objective

Halal certification transforms local products into globally trusted commodities, creating export opportunities, revenue streams, and brand recognition for Muslim communities. This chapter provides a strategic framework for Halal product development, certification, and global market penetration.

Why Halal Certification & Niche Markets Matter

Global Market Access: Halal consumers exceed **1.9+ billion people** worldwide

Revenue Expansion: Certified products command premium pricing and export contracts

Cultural Identity & Trust: Certification builds authenticity, traceability, and consumer confidence

Local Economic Growth: Supports SMEs, agriculture, and neighborhood production hubs

Innovation in Niche Sectors: Cosmetics, pharmaceuticals, and lifestyle products with Halal compliance

Case Examples

- Malaysia & UAE: Global leaders in Halal-certified food exports
- Indonesia: Halal cosmetics integrated with e-commerce exports
- Turkey: Halal logistics and certification frameworks linking Europe and Asia

Step 1 — Map Halal Market Opportunities

Focus Areas

- **Food & Beverage:** Meat, dairy, packaged foods, beverages
- **Cosmetics & Pharmaceuticals:** Skincare, supplements, personal care
- **Fashion & Lifestyle:** Modest wear, accessories, lifestyle goods
- **Export Channels:** E-commerce, distributors, retail partnerships
- **Local Production:** SMEs, cooperatives, and neighborhood food hubs

Checklist — Halal Readiness Audit

- Ingredient and supply chain compliance
- Slaughter, hygiene, and handling process verification
- Packaging, labeling, and traceability systems
- Identification of export-ready products
- Target market certification requirements

Step 2 — Strategic Approach

Strategy

Build an integrated **Halal product ecosystem** connecting certification, production, branding, and global distribution.

Core Pillars

1. Certification Infrastructure

- Establish local/national Halal certification authorities
- Align with international standards for global recognition
- Regular audits and transparent labeling systems

2. Product Development & Standardization

- Train producers in Halal-compliant processes
- Implement quality assurance and hygiene protocols

- Integrate sustainable and ethical production practices

3. Market Access & Export Strategy

- Target markets: Middle East, Southeast Asia, Europe, North America
- Partner with distributors, retailers, and trade expos
- Adapt packaging and branding for international consumers

4. Local Producer Empowerment

- Training and funding for SMEs and cooperatives
- Integration with neighborhood markets and city supply chains
- Encourage innovation in high-value Halal niches

5. Digital Platforms & E-Commerce

- Online Halal marketplaces and export portals
- Logistics and international shipping support
- Social media marketing emphasizing certification and origin

Step 3 — Halal Market Development Framework Blueprint
Purpose

Create a scalable roadmap for Halal production, certification, and export growth.

Components

- **Certification Authorities:** Compliance bodies, auditors, verification systems
- **Producer Training & SME Support:** Workshops, mentorship, funding
- **Market Access Channels:** Retail, e-commerce, export

networks

- **Branding & Consumer Education:** Trust signals, packaging, awareness campaigns
- **Monitoring & Metrics:** Compliance, export volumes, revenue, customer trust

Visual Concept

Halal Market Development Framework
├── Certification Authorities
├── Producer Training & SME Support
├── Market Access & Distribution
├── Branding & Consumer Education
└── Monitoring & Metrics

Step 4 — Business Canvas Application

Block	Details
Value Proposition	Trusted, certified Halal products for global and domestic markets
Key Activities	Certification, production oversight, export logistics, marketing
Key Resources	Certification bodies, trained producers, digital platforms, logistics networks
Key Partners	Halal certifiers, SMEs, cooperatives, exporters, e-commerce platforms
Revenue Streams	Domestic sales, export contracts, certification fees, partnerships
Customer Segments	Halal-conscious consumers, retailers, distributors
Channels	Online marketplaces, retail chains, export networks, trade fairs
Customer Relationships	Trust-based, transparent, certification-driven
Cost Structure	Certification, production support, logistics, marketing
Metrics	Certified products, export revenue, global market penetration

Step 5 — Risk Assessment & Mitigation

Risk	Impact	Mitigation
Non-compliance with Halal standards	High	SOPs, audits, certification training
Export barriers/tariffs	Medium	Trade agreements, export advisory
Low market visibility	Medium	Digital marketing, trade fairs
Infrastructure bottlenecks	Medium	Shared production hubs, cooperative networks
Consumer trust issues	High	Transparent labeling and verified certification

Step 6 — Implementation Timeline

Phase	Activities	Outcome
Phase 1 (0–6 months)	Establish certification bodies, audit producers	Certified baseline products
Phase 2 (6–12 months)	Producer training, launch e-commerce, domestic sales	Early revenue & brand awareness
Phase 3 (1–3 years)	Expand exports, trade fairs, scale production	International revenue growth
Phase 4 (3–5 years)	Global distribution, product innovation, brand leadership	Sustainable Halal market ecosystem

Step 7 — Community and Cultural Integration

- Promote local Halal ingredients and artisanal production
- Encourage youth and women-led Halal startups
- Link Halal production with tourism (food festivals, cultural markets)
- Ensure transparency, community participation, and trust in certification systems

Conclusion

Halal certification and niche markets represent a **powerful, globally scalable economic engine**.

By:

- Establishing strong certification and compliance frameworks
- Empowering SMEs and cooperatives with training and funding
- Connecting products to domestic and international markets
- Leveraging digital platforms for global outreach

Muslim communities can generate **sustainable revenue, global brand recognition, and culturally aligned economic growth**, transforming local production into internationally trusted and competitive industries.

Chapter 25 — Green Spaces and Sustainable Urban Design

Objective

Green spaces and sustainable urban design enhance quality of life, environmental resilience, and economic opportunity. By integrating parks, urban farms, eco-tourism, and green rooftops, neighborhoods and cities can generate revenue, foster community engagement, and contribute to climate goals.

Why Green Spaces & Sustainable Design Matter

Economic Benefits

Urban farms, eco-tourism, landscaping services, and green infrastructure create jobs and new revenue streams.

Environmental Impact

Reduced pollution, improved air quality, storm water management, biodiversity conservation, and urban cooling.

Social Cohesion

Parks, gardens, and eco-events provide shared spaces for recreation, wellness, and community bonding.

Urban Resilience

Green rooftops, tree canopies, and water systems reduce heat islands, flooding risk, and climate vulnerability.

Revenue Generation

Income from produce sales, eco-tourism, events, sponsorships, and carbon credit programs.

Case Examples

- **Singapore**: Vertical gardens, green rooftops, and urban biodiversity corridors improve livability and attract eco-tourism.
- **Dubai & Abu Dhabi**: Commercial developments integrate

rooftop farms and green design into modern architecture.

- **Istanbul**: Community gardens and eco-parks linked with tourism and cultural activities.

Step 1 — Map Neighborhood Green Opportunities
Focus Areas

- **Parks & Recreational Areas**: Walking trails, playgrounds, open-air community zones
- **Urban Farms & Community Gardens**: Food production, agri-tourism, and education
- **Eco-Tourism Circuits**: Green tours, environmental workshops, sustainable architecture tours
- **Green Roofs & Vertical Gardens**: Building insulation, cooling, and aesthetics
- **Carbon Credit Programs**: Monetizing sustainability through measurable emission reductions

Checklist — Sustainability Readiness

- Land and rooftop mapping completed
- Soil testing and irrigation systems planned
- Community engagement and volunteer programs initiated
- Revenue streams identified (produce, events, credits)
- Compliance with environmental and zoning regulations

Step 2 — Strategic Approach
1. Community Gardens & Urban Farms

- Allocate shared plots and cooperative farming zones
- Train residents in composting, organic farming, and water efficiency
- Sell produce through local markets, digital platforms, and

farm-to-table partnerships

2. Eco-Tourism Development

- Develop walking tours, rooftop gardens, and eco-festivals
- Organize sustainability workshops and environmental education programs
- Partner with hotels, travel agencies, and cultural centers

3. Green Infrastructure Integration

- Install green rooftops and vertical gardens
- Develop solar-lit parks and water recycling systems
- Promote sustainable architecture as part of neighborhood branding

4. Carbon Credit Monetization

- Measure emissions reduction through green coverage
- Partner with verification agencies for carbon certification
- Sell credits to corporations or climate funds

5. Policy & Governance Facilitation

- Simplify permits and approvals for green installations
- Offer tax incentives and grants for eco-projects
- Partner with NGOs, universities, and sustainability departments

Step 3 — Neighborhood Sustainability Map Blueprint

Purpose: A comprehensive layout for integrating green spaces and sustainable systems.

Components

- Parks & Recreation Zones
- Urban Farms & Community Gardens
- Green Rooftops & Vertical Gardens
- Eco-Tourism Circuits & Event Spaces
- Water, Waste & Resource Management Systems
- Monitoring, Revenue & Carbon Credit Tracking

Neighborhood Sustainability Map
├── Parks & Recreation Zones
├── Urban Farms & Community Gardens
├── Green Rooftops & Vertical Gardens
├── Eco-Tourism Circuits & Events
└── Monitoring, Revenue & Carbon Credit Tracking

Step 4 — Business Canvas Application

Block	Details
Value Proposition	Sustainable, green, revenue-generating neighborhood ecosystems
Key Activities	Urban farming, eco-events, park management, green construction, carbon credit programs
Key Resources	Land, green technology, horticulture experts, volunteers
Key Partners	NGOs, municipalities, tourism operators, universities
Revenue Streams	Produce sales, eco-tourism tickets, carbon credits, sponsorships
Customer Segments	Residents, tourists, businesses, corporate partners
Channels	Markets, eco-events, online platforms, tours
Customer Relationships	Participatory, educational, community-driven
Cost Structure	Infrastructure, maintenance, training, marketing
Metrics	Green coverage %, yield, attendance, carbon credits, engagement

Step 5 — Risk Assessment & Mitigation

Risk	Impact	Mitigation
Low community engagement	High	Volunteer programs, co-design workshops
Poor maintenance	Medium	Local stewardship committees and monitoring dashboards
Low eco-event revenue	Medium	Tourism partnerships and bundled experiences
Regulatory barriers	Medium	Early consultation and compliance frameworks
Climate risks (drought/flooding)	High	Drought-resistant plants, irrigation, rainwater harvesting

Step 6 — Implementation Timeline

Phase	Activities	Outcome
Phase 1 (0–6 months)	Mapping, planning, engagement	Baseline readiness
Phase 2 (6–12 months)	Pilot gardens, initial eco-events	Early revenue & participation
Phase 3 (1–3 years)	Expand rooftops, tourism, carbon credits	Revenue growth & environmental impact
Phase 4 (3–5 years)	Integrated city-level green ecosystem	Long-term sustainability & prosperity

Step 7 — Community and Cultural Integration

- Promote native and culturally meaningful plant species
- Engage schools, youth, and women-led groups
- Integrate Halal food production into urban farms
- Use green spaces for festivals, markets, and community gatherings
- Position neighborhoods as models of sustainable Muslim urban living

Conclusion

Green spaces and sustainable urban design are **economic engines, social connectors, and environmental safeguards**.

By:

- Developing community gardens, urban farms, and eco-tourism
- Monetizing green initiatives through produce, events, and carbon credits
- Engaging residents and local businesses
- Integrating neighborhood planning with city sustainability policies

Communities can build **resilient, vibrant, and economically self-sustaining urban ecosystems** that align with both environmental responsibility and cultural values.

Chapter 26 — Local Skills and Workforce Mapping

Objective

A community's human capital is its most valuable asset. Aligning resident skills with local and regional economic demand ensures employment, productivity, and sustainable growth. This chapter provides a strategic framework for mapping skills, developing workforce potential, and connecting labor with economic opportunities.

Why Skills and Workforce Mapping Matter

Maximized Employment

Matching resident skills with market needs reduces unemployment and underemployment.

Economic Growth

A skilled workforce increases productivity, strengthens SMEs, and attracts domestic and foreign investment.

Social Cohesion

Inclusive employment programs empower youth, women, and marginalized groups, strengthening community stability.

Entrepreneurial Ecosystems

Skills mapping identifies future entrepreneurs, cooperative leaders, and local service providers.

Revenue Generation

Higher employment and productivity increase household income, local consumption, and tax base.

Case Examples

- **Singapore Skills Future**: National initiative aligning workforce skills with future economic demands.
- **Dubai Human Capital Development Programs**: Vocational

and SME-integrated training aligned with free zone industries.

- **Istanbul Neighborhood Skills Mapping**: Local trade skills connected to tourism, crafts, and service sectors.

Step 1 — Map Neighborhood & City Skills
Focus Areas

- **Resident Skills Audit**
  Education, vocational, technical, artisanal, and soft skills
- **Industry & Market Demand Analysis**
  Mapping SMEs, cooperatives, city industries, and growth sectors
- **Employment & Entrepreneurial Potential**
  Identifying pathways into jobs, self-employment, and cooperatives
- **Future Skill Gaps**
  Digital literacy, AI tools, e-commerce, renewable energy, logistics, healthcare support

Checklist — Workforce Mapping

- Resident skill database (formal and informal skills)
- Local and regional industry demand mapping
- Skill-to-job matching framework
- Certification and qualification mapping
- Training institutions and program capacity assessment

Step 2 — Strategic Approach
1. Vocational Training & Apprenticeships

- Technical trades, services, digital work, and Halal food

production
- Partnerships with SMEs and local businesses for apprenticeship pipelines
- Modular, flexible learning formats for youth, women, and part-time learners

2. Skill Certification & Recognition

- Standardized certification for formal and informal skills
- Local accreditation aligned with national and international standards
- Recognition programs to promote lifelong learning

3. Employment & Placement Platforms

- Digital job portals and local employment hubs
- Integration with city/state workforce systems
- Career counseling, mentorship, and placement services

4. Entrepreneurial Pathways

- Identify skills suitable for micro-enterprises and cooperatives
- Provide incubation, mentorship, and microfinance
- Integrate entrepreneurs into neighborhood markets, e-commerce, and export ecosystems

5. Policy & Institutional Support

- Subsidized training programs
- Partnerships with schools, universities, NGOs, and vocational institutes
- Workforce monitoring aligned with city and state economic development strategies

Step 3 — Neighborhood Workforce Development Plan Blueprint

Purpose: A structured, scalable framework to map, develop, and deploy local skills.

Components

- Skills Audit & Database
- Industry Mapping & Demand Alignment
- Training & Certification Programs
- Employment & Apprenticeship Placement
- Monitoring & Metrics Dashboard

```
Neighborhood Workforce Development Plan
├─ Skills Audit & Database
├─ Industry Mapping & Demand Alignment
├─ Training & Certification Programs
├─ Employment & Apprenticeship Placement
└─ Monitoring & Metrics Dashboard
```

Step 4 — Business Canvas Application

Block	Details
Value Proposition	Skilled, employable, and entrepreneurial workforce aligned with economic demand
Key Activities	Skills mapping, training, certification, job placement, entrepreneurship development
Key Resources	Human capital, training centers, mentors, digital platforms
Key Partners	Vocational institutes, SMEs, cooperatives, city workforce agencies, NGOs
Revenue Streams	Training fees, certification fees, cooperative profit share, increased local income
Customer Segments	Residents, businesses, cooperatives, city planners
Channels	Training centers, online platforms, apprenticeships, cooperative hubs
Customer Relationships	Mentorship-based, participatory, continuous development
Cost Structure	Training facilities, staff, digital infrastructure, certification processes
Metrics	Residents trained, jobs filled, income growth, entrepreneurship rate, skill-job alignment

Step 5 — Risk Assessment & Mitigation

Risk	Impact	Mitigation
Low participation in training	Medium	Awareness campaigns, flexible schedules, stipends
Skill mismatch with demand	High	Continuous industry mapping, adaptive curricula
Funding constraints	Medium	Subsidies, NGO funding, cooperative investment models
Low training quality	Medium	Standardized certification, instructor evaluation
Migration of skilled workers	Medium	Local job creation, entrepreneurship incentives, retention programs

Step 6 — Implementation Timeline

Phase	Activities	Outcome
Phase 1 (0–3 months)	Skills audit, industry mapping, training design	Workforce baseline established
Phase 2 (3–9 months)	Launch training, apprenticeships, certification	Initial job placements
Phase 3 (1–2 years)	Expand digital training and placement platforms	Increased employment and enterprise creation
Phase 4 (2–5 years)	Continuous alignment with economic policy	Self-sustaining workforce ecosystem

Step 7 — Community and Cultural Integration

- Promote locally relevant skills such as crafts, Halal food production, cultural tourism, and digital services
- Prioritize inclusion of youth, women, and underserved groups
- Link workforce development with neighborhood cooperatives and economic hubs

- Encourage future-oriented sectors: renewable energy, fin tech, sustainable construction, logistics

Conclusion

Local skills and workforce mapping form the **foundation of sustainable economic development**.

By:

- Conducting comprehensive skills audits and demand mapping
- Delivering vocational training, apprenticeships, and certification
- Linking skills to employment, entrepreneurship, and cooperatives
- Leveraging digital platforms for workforce matching

Communities can **maximize human potential, generate income, attract investment, and build resilient, self-reliant local economies** aligned with long-term growth and social stability.

Chapter 27 — Community Events and Cultural Festivals

Objective

Community events and cultural festivals celebrate heritage, strengthen social bonds, and generate revenue. When strategically designed, these activities transform neighborhoods into vibrant economic, cultural, and tourism hubs—creating opportunities for local businesses, artisans, and service providers.

Why Community Events & Cultural Festivals Matter

Revenue Generation

Ticket sales, vendor fees, sponsorships, concessions, and merchandise generate direct income streams.

Economic Multipliers

Events stimulate nearby markets, restaurants, transport, and accommodation services.

Cultural Preservation

Festivals preserve heritage, traditions, crafts, and local identity across generations.

Social Cohesion

Community participation fosters pride, volunteerism, and cross-generational engagement.

Tourism & Place Branding

Events position neighborhoods as cultural destinations, attracting domestic and international visitors.

Case Examples

- **Fez Festival of World Sacred Music** — Blends spiritual music, heritage, and tourism to generate revenue and global visibility
- **Istanbul International Festival** — Integrates concerts, art,

and local markets to boost SMEs and artisans

- **Dubai Global Village** — Large-scale cultural expo supporting small businesses and global trade

Step 1 — Plan Neighborhood Events & Festivals

Focus Areas

Event Types

Cultural festivals, seasonal fairs, night markets, food bazaars, art exhibitions, and religious celebrations

Target Audience

Residents, tourists, families, students, and cultural enthusiasts

Revenue Streams

Ticketing, vendor fees, sponsorships, grants, concessions, merchandise

Public–Private Partnerships

Local businesses, NGOs, schools, mosques, and cultural institutions

Digital Presence

Online ticketing, social media campaigns, event apps, influencer marketing

Checklist — Event Readiness

- Annual calendar with key seasonal and cultural dates
- Vendor registry, contracts, and compliance standards
- Marketing campaigns scheduled (digital + offline)
- Venue permits, insurance, safety, and accessibility planning
- Logistics: transport, parking, sanitation, waste management

Step 2 — Strategic Approach

1. Ticketing & Admission Strategy

- Tiered pricing (residents, tourists, family packages, VIP experiences)

- Bundled experiences: food tastings, craft workshops, guided tours
- Early-bird and group discounts to boost attendance

2. Vendor & Marketplace Management

- Local artisans, SMEs, Halal food vendors, and cultural exhibitors
- Transparent vendor fees and quality standards
- Incentives for innovation, repeat participation, and product diversity

3. Sponsorship & Partnerships

- Corporate sponsorships, NGO grants, municipal funding
- Co-branded events and workshops
- Revenue-sharing agreements with partners

4. Marketing & Cultural Branding

- Digital campaigns: social media, video storytelling, influencer collaborations
- Local promotion: schools, mosques, community centers, local media
- Narrative-driven branding centered on heritage and identity

5. Integration with Local Economy

- Promote nearby accommodations, restaurants, and transport services
- Encourage local shopping through festival-linked promotions
- Showcase neighborhood products (Halal foods, crafts, fashion, digital services)

Step 3 — Neighborhood Cultural Economy Plan Blueprint

Purpose: Establish a structured, revenue-generating cultural ecosystem anchored in recurring events.

Components

- Event Calendar & Seasonal Programming
- Vendor & Stakeholder Engagement System
- Revenue & Financial Tracking Model
- Marketing & Promotion Framework
- Monitoring & Impact Metrics Dashboard

```
Neighborhood Cultural Economy Plan
├── Event Calendar & Scheduling
├── Vendor & Stakeholder Engagement
├── Revenue Models & Financial Tracking
├── Marketing & Promotion
└── Monitoring & Impact Metrics
```

Step 4 — Business Canvas Application

Block	Details
Value Proposition	Vibrant, culturally rich experiences that generate revenue and preserve heritage
Key Activities	Event planning, vendor coordination, marketing, sponsorship management
Key Resources	Venues, cultural assets, volunteers, logistics infrastructure
Key Partners	Local businesses, NGOs, cultural institutions, sponsors, city authorities
Revenue Streams	Ticket sales, vendor fees, sponsorships, concessions, merchandise
Customer Segments	Residents, tourists, students, cultural audiences
Channels	Online platforms, ticketing apps, social media, community networks
Customer Relationships	Interactive, participatory, community-driven
Cost Structure	Venue rental, marketing, staff, logistics, security, permits
Metrics	Attendance, revenue, vendor performance, local business impact, satisfaction

Step 5 — Risk Assessment & Mitigation

Risk	Impact	Mitigation
Low attendance	Medium	Early marketing, partnerships, community outreach
Vendor dissatisfaction	Medium	Transparent policies, fair pricing, feedback channels
Weather disruptions	High	Covered venues, contingency plans, event insurance
Safety & security issues	High	Crowd management, trained staff, emergency response plans
Financial shortfall	Medium	Diversified sponsorship, contingency budgets, phased scaling

Step 6 — Implementation Timeline

Phase	Activities	Outcome
Phase 1 (0–3 months)	Define events, secure venues, recruit vendors and sponsors	Event roadmap established
Phase 2 (3–6 months)	Launch marketing, finalize logistics, open ticketing	Pre-event awareness and revenue
Phase 3 (6–12 months)	Host pilot events, collect feedback, optimize operations	Refined and scalable model
Phase 4 (1–3 years)	Expand festivals, integrate tourism and sponsorships	Sustainable cultural economy ecosystem

Step 7 — Community and Cultural Integration

- Encourage residents to participate in planning, volunteering, and performance
- Showcase local crafts, heritage, cuisine, and storytelling traditions
- Ensure Halal-compliant food and culturally aligned services
- Promote youth and women-led businesses within festivals
- Measure social and economic impact to refine future events

Conclusion

Community events and cultural festivals are **powerful engines of local economic growth and cultural preservation.**

By:

- Creating structured, recurring event calendars
- Engaging local vendors, artisans, and sponsors
- Leveraging digital marketing and tourism networks
- Integrating events with neighborhood businesses and identity

Communities can **generate revenue, strengthen social cohesion, preserve cultural heritage, and position themselves as vibrant, resilient, and economically dynamic cultural destinations.**

Chapter 28 — Business Canvas for Neighborhoods, Cities, and States

Objective

The **Business Model Canvas (BMC)** is a strategic management framework that enables communities, cities, and states to visualize, design, and optimize their economic and social ecosystems.

When applied at multiple scales, the canvas ensures that **value creation, resource utilization, governance, and revenue generation are aligned vertically—from neighborhood initiatives to national strategy.**

Why a Multi-Scale Business Canvas Matters

Holistic Planning

Connect micro-level (neighborhood) initiatives with macro-level (city and state) strategies.

Efficiency & Transparency

Identify redundancies, reduce waste, optimize funding, and monitor KPIs clearly.

Revenue Maximization

Align activities, partnerships, and channels to capture all available income streams.

Cultural & Social Integration

Ensure economic systems respect heritage, community welfare, and Islamic values.

Resilience & Adaptability

Rapidly adjust to policy shifts, economic volatility, and technological disruption.

Case Examples

- **Smart Nation Singapore** — Integrates neighborhood services with city-wide digital and economic strategy

- **Expo 2020 Dubai** — Multi-level economic planning aligned event legacy with city and national goals
- **Istanbul Metropolitan Municipality** — Connects neighborhood cooperatives with tourism and industrial development strategies

Step 1 — Apply Business Canvas Principles at Every Scale

1. Neighborhood Level

Focus: Micro-enterprises, cooperatives, events, urban farms, workforce development

Value Proposition:

Community well-being, local income generation, cultural preservation, social cohesion

2. City Level

Focus: Urban planning, SMEs, tourism, creative economy, smart infrastructure

Value Proposition:

Vibrant economy, sustainable services, investor attraction, livability

3. State/National Level

Focus: Trade, energy, large-scale infrastructure, education, healthcare, digital economy

Value Proposition:

Fiscal self-sufficiency, employment growth, global competitiveness

Step 2 — Strategic Approach

Strategy

Develop a **layered, integrated Business Model Canvas** linking:

Neighborhood → City → State/National

1. Workshops & Stakeholder Validation

- Conduct BMC workshops at each level
- Engage residents, businesses, cooperatives, policymakers, and

investors
- Validate value propositions, revenue streams, and KPIs

2. Revenue & Cost Alignment
Neighborhood Revenue

- Local sales
- Events and marketplaces
- Cooperative profits
- Micro-enterprise services

City Revenue

- Property taxes
- Business permits
- Tourism fees
- Public-private partnerships

State/National Revenue

- Exports
- Trade taxes
- Energy revenues
- Large-scale industries

3. KPI Mapping
Track across scales:

- Employment rate
- Revenue growth
- Investment inflow
- Social participation
- Cultural engagement

- Infrastructure efficiency

4. Iterative Optimization

- Use neighborhood data to refine city strategy
- Use city metrics to inform state-level policy
- Continuously adjust partnerships and resource allocation

Step 3 — Checklist for Multi-Level Business Canvas

Step	Task
1	Identify stakeholders at each scale
2	Map value propositions for neighborhood, city, state
3	Identify key activities and resources
4	Determine partnerships and collaboration networks
5	Define revenue streams and cost structures
6	Establish customer relationships and channels
7	Set measurable KPIs
8	Conduct validation workshops
9	Integrate canvases vertically
10	Implement iterative review cycles

Step 4 — Layered Business Canvas Blueprint

```
Layered Business Canvas
├── Neighborhood Level
│   ├── Value Proposition
│   ├── Key Activities
│   ├── Key Resources
│   ├── Partners
│   ├── Revenue Streams
│   ├── Cost Structure
│   ├── Customer Segments
│   ├── Channels
│   └── Metrics/KPIs
│
```

```
├─ City Level
│  ├─ Value Proposition
│  ├─ Key Activities
│  ├─ Key Resources
│  ├─ Partners
│  ├─ Revenue Streams
│  ├─ Cost Structure
│  ├─ Customer Segments
│  ├─ Channels
│  └─ Metrics/KPIs
└─ State/National Level
├─ Value Proposition
├─ Key Activities
├─ Key Resources
├─ Partners
├─ Revenue Streams
├─ Cost Structure
├─ Customer Segments
├─ Channels
└─ Metrics/KPIs
```

Step 5 — Business Canvas at Each Scale

A. Neighborhood Canvas Example

Value Proposition

Vibrant local economy rooted in culture and cooperation

Key Activities

Micro-entrepreneurship, festivals, urban farms, skills training

Key Resources

Human capital, public spaces, cooperative funds

Revenue Streams

Local sales, ticketed events, cooperative profits

KPIs

Employment rate, income growth, participation level, satisfaction index

B. City Canvas Example

Value Proposition

Smart, sustainable city with economic diversity

Key Activities

Urban planning, SME support, tourism development

Key Resources

Transport networks, municipal assets, tech infrastructure

Revenue Streams

Property taxes, permits, tourism income, PPP investments

KPIs

Investment inflow, GDP contribution, quality-of-life index

C. State/National Canvas Example

Value Proposition

Globally competitive, fiscally sovereign economy

Key Activities

Trade, energy, education, digital governance

Key Resources

Natural resources, human capital, infrastructure

Revenue Streams

Taxes, exports, energy production, sovereign investments

KPIs

GDP growth, export volume, fiscal balance, employment

Step 6 — Risk Assessment & Mitigation

Risk	Impact	Mitigation
Misalignment across scales	High	Integrated dashboards, cross-level coordination councils
Revenue leakage	Medium	Transparent accounting, digital monitoring
Stakeholder resistance	Medium	Early engagement, co-design workshops
Rapid tech/ economic shifts	High	Adaptive planning, real-time data
Skill gaps	Medium	Workforce programs linked to canvas insights

Step 7 — Implementation Timeline

Phase	Activities	Outcome
Phase 1 (0–3 months)	Conduct workshops, map neighborhood canvases	Baseline BMC established
Phase 2 (3–6 months)	Align neighborhood & city canvases	Operational integration
Phase 3 (6–12 months)	Integrate city & state strategies	Multi-scale alignment
Phase 4 (1–3 years)	Implement KPIs, continuous review & optimization	Fully adaptive BMC system

Step 8 — Conclusion

A layered Business Model Canvas transforms neighborhoods, cities, and states into **aligned, revenue-generating, and resilient ecosystems.**

By:

- Mapping value propositions and revenue streams at every scale
- Vertically integrating local, city, and national strategies
- Monitoring performance through shared KPIs

- Engaging public, private, and community stakeholders

Communities can create **economically strong, culturally grounded, and strategically coordinated systems** that sustain prosperity across generations.

Chapter 29 — Investment, Grants, and International Aid

Objective

Attracting **ethical, sustainable, and development-focused funding** is essential for neighborhoods, cities, and states to grow **without compromising cultural values or social cohesion**.

This chapter provides a strategic framework to mobilize **multi-source finance**—including grants, diaspora investment, public-private partnerships, and international aid—to support **economic growth, infrastructure, social services, and entrepreneurship**.

Why Multi-Source Funding Matters

Diversified Revenue Streams

Reduces reliance on taxation or single-industry economies.

Catalyst for Development

Finances infrastructure, education, healthcare, SMEs, and innovation.

Global Connectivity

Engages diaspora communities, NGOs, investors, and development institutions.

Sustainability & Accountability

Ethical funding ensures long-term alignment with Islamic and community values.

Economic Multipliers

Funding generates jobs, stimulates SMEs, and strengthens local markets.

Case Examples

- Dubai development projects funded through global investors and diaspora participation
- Indonesia village grant programs supporting community-led

infrastructure and enterprises
- Morocco renewable energy programs financed through international development partnerships

Key institutions often involved include:

- **United Nations Development Programme (UNDP)**
- **World Bank**
- **Islamic Development Bank**

Step 1 — Map Funding Sources
1. International Development Grants
Sources:

- UN agencies
- Development banks
- Regional development funds

Priority sectors:

- Energy & climate
- Education
- Healthcare
- Digital economy
- Infrastructure

2. Diaspora Investment
Strategy:

- Engage expatriate Muslims to invest in hometown development
- Create **cooperative investment vehicles and sukuk-style funds**

- Provide transparent reporting and returns

3. Public-Private Partnerships (PPP)**
Applications:

- Infrastructure
- Transport
- Healthcare & education
- Digital infrastructure

Mechanism:

- Revenue sharing
- Concessions
- Performance-based contracts

4. NGOs & Development Organizations

- Skill development programs
- Social welfare initiatives
- Community capacity building

5. Ethical Crowd funding & Social Impact Funds

- Citizen participation in local development
- Micro-investment platforms
- Impact-based returns and reporting

Step 2 — Strategic Approach
Strategy

Develop a **transparent, multi-source funding system** aligned with economic priorities and cultural values.

A. Grant Application Framework

1. Conduct funding eligibility audits
2. Identify aligned grant programs
3. Draft proposals with:
    - Measurable impact
    - Clear budgets
    - Implementation timelines
4. Build partnerships with implementing agencies

B. Diaspora Engagement Strategy

- Establish **trust through transparency**
- Provide:
    - Profit-sharing models
    - Community co-ownership
    - Recognition programs
- Promote investment via:
    - Mosques
    - Community networks
    - International forums

C. PPP Development Framework

- Transparent bidding and contracting
- Align projects with local cultural and social goals
- Continuous performance monitoring
- Clear dispute resolution mechanisms

D. Compliance & Accountability

- Financial dashboards
- Audit systems
- Legal compliance tracking
- KPI-based monitoring

Step 3 — Multi-Source Funding Checklist

Task	Description
Funding Eligibility Audit	Identify grants, PPPs, diaspora opportunities
Proposal Drafting	Budget, timeline, KPIs, expected outcomes
Legal Compliance	Regulatory approval for foreign funding
Stakeholder Engagement	NGOs, investors, government, community
Risk Assessment	Financial, political, reputational risks
Funding Dashboard	Track applications, approvals, utilization

Step 4 — Multi-Source Funding Framework Blueprint

```
Multi-Source Funding Framework
├─ Funding Source Mapping
│  ├─ International Grants
│  ├─ Diaspora Investment
│  ├─ PPP Projects
│  ├─ NGO Partnerships
│  └─ Crowd funding Platforms
├─ Project Prioritization & Selection
├─ Proposal & Application Management
├─ Compliance & Reporting Systems
└─ Impact Evaluation & Continuous Improvement
```

Step 5 — Business Canvas Application

Value Proposition

Ethical, transparent, and diversified funding enabling sustainable development

Key Activities

Grant applications, diaspora investment programs, PPP management, compliance tracking

Key Resources

Grant writers, financial experts, legal teams, project managers, digital dashboards

Key Partners

Development agencies, diaspora networks, private investors, NGOs, government bodies

Revenue Streams

Grants, capital investment, PPP revenues, crowd funding contributions

Customer Segments

Residents, SMEs, cooperatives, city/state authorities

Channels

Investor forums, online platforms, development expos, community meetings

Customer Relationships

Trust-based, transparent, participatory

Cost Structure

Administration, compliance, reporting, stakeholder engagement

KPIs

- Funding secured
- Projects completed
- Employment generated
- Social impact achieved

Step 6 — Risk Assessment & Mitigation

Risk	Impact	Mitigation
Grant rejection	Medium	Professional proposal design, early screening
Diaspora withdrawal	Medium	Regular updates, transparent reporting
PPP delays	High	Strict contracts, milestone tracking
Compliance failure	High	Legal oversight, audit systems
Overdependence on external funds	Medium	Balance with local revenue & cooperative finance

Step 7 — Implementation Timeline

Phase	Activities	Outcome
Phase 1 (0–3 months)	Identify funding sources & pipeline	Funding strategy ready
Phase 2 (3–6 months)	Submit proposals & engage diaspora	Initial capital inflow
Phase 3 (6–12 months)	Launch projects & reporting systems	Visible impact & credibility
Phase 4 (1–3 years)	Scale funding ecosystem & replicate models	Sustainable financing system

Step 8 — Community Integration & Cultural Alignment

- Align all funding with **Islamic ethical principles**
- Promote **Halal-compliant investments and contracts**
- Engage residents in planning, monitoring, and feedback
- Use funding to strengthen:
    - Skills development
    - SMEs and cooperatives
    - Infrastructure
    - Cultural programs

Conclusion

A **multi-source funding framework** enables communities to grow **financially, socially, and culturally—without losing identity or autonomy.**

By:

- Mobilizing grants, diaspora capital, PPPs, and NGOs
- Ensuring transparency, accountability, and ethical governance
- Aligning funding with real community needs
- Integrating local, city, and national development strategies

Neighborhoods, cities, and states can unlock **long-term prosperity, resilience, and self-reliant growth**, creating **economically strong and culturally grounded Muslim societies.**

Chapter 30 — Technology and Digital Transformation

Objective

Technology and digital transformation are powerful levers for economic growth, governance efficiency, and citizen engagement. By leveraging **e-governance, fin tech, smart logistics, and online marketplaces**, neighborhoods, cities, and states can enhance revenue streams, improve service delivery, and strengthen social cohesion.

Why Technology Matters

Efficiency & Cost Reduction

Automation, paperless transactions, and digital monitoring reduce administrative overhead and corruption risks.

New Revenue Streams

Digital marketplaces, fin tech platforms, subscription services, and e-governance fees create new income channels.

Citizen Engagement & Transparency

Digital platforms increase participation, trust, and accountability.

Data-Driven Decision Making

Analytics enable predictive planning, resource optimization, and risk mitigation.

Global Competitiveness

Technology attracts investors, startups, and skilled talent.

Global Case References

- Estonia's digital governance ecosystem enables seamless business registration, taxation, and citizen services.
- Dubai's smart city model integrates AI, IoT, and digital governance across municipal systems.
- Singapore's digital economy platforms connect logistics, commerce, and financial systems into a unified ecosystem.

Step 1 — Plan Digital Transformation
Core Focus Areas
1. E-Governance

- Digitize permits, licensing, taxation, utilities, and grievance systems
- Single-window service platforms to eliminate bureaucratic delays

2. Fin tech Ecosystems

- Mobile payments, digital wallets, microfinance, and crowd funding
- Enable diaspora investments and cooperative finance

3. Digital Marketplaces

- E-commerce for local products, Halal goods, crafts, and services
- Link SMEs to national and global buyers

4. Smart Logistics & Supply Chains

- IoT-enabled inventory, delivery tracking, and transport optimization
- Integrated distribution networks from neighborhood to state level

5. Digital Skills & Workforce Development

- Coding, IT services, e-commerce, and digital entrepreneurship
- Partnerships with universities and training institutions

Step 2 — Strategic Approach
Neighborhood & City Digital Integration Strategy
Infrastructure Development

- High-speed broadband, data centers, cloud computing, IoT systems
- Backup servers and disaster recovery mechanisms

Cyber security & Data Protection

- Encryption protocols, firewalls, identity management
- Data privacy regulations and compliance audits

Digital Inclusion

- Accessible, multilingual platforms
- Affordable internet access and community digital centers

Process Automation

- Automated tax systems, permits, compliance monitoring
- AI-driven analytics for governance decisions

Revenue Integration

- Connect fin tech and e-governance platforms with public revenue dashboards
- Use transaction data to optimize economic policies

Step 3 — Digital Transformation Checklist

- IT infrastructure and cloud readiness audit
- Cyber security framework and incident response plan
- Workforce digital training programs

- Deployment of e-governance and fin tech platforms
- Integration with taxation and revenue systems
- Stakeholder engagement (citizens, SMEs, government, tech firms)
- KPI dashboards for monitoring adoption and performance

Step 4 — Digital Integration Framework Blueprint

Neighborhood & City Digital Integration Plan

```
├── IT Infrastructure & Cloud Systems
├── E-Governance Platforms
├── Fin tech & Payment Ecosystems
├── Digital Marketplaces & E-Commerce
├── Smart Logistics & Supply Chains
├── Data Analytics & Decision Systems
├── Cyber security & Regulatory Compliance
└── Skills Development & Digital Literacy
```

Step 5 — Business Model Canvas

Block	Details
Value Proposition	Efficient governance, digital commerce, economic empowerment
Key Activities	Platform development, automation, analytics, Cyber security
Key Resources	IT infrastructure, cloud systems, data analytics, skilled workforce
Key Partners	Tech firms, universities, fin tech providers, government agencies
Revenue Streams	Service fees, transaction commissions, digital sales, efficiency savings
Cost Structure	Infrastructure, maintenance, Cyber security, training
Customer Segments	Citizens, SMEs, investors, tourists
Channels	Mobile apps, portals, kiosks, social media
Customer Relationships	Transparent, user-friendly, responsive
KPIs	Platform adoption, transactions, service speed, revenue generated

Step 6 — Risk Assessment & Mitigation

Risk	Impact	Mitigation
Cyber security breaches	High	Encryption, audits, security protocols
Digital divide	Medium	Subsidized access, community training
System downtime	High	Redundant infrastructure, disaster recovery
Low adoption	Medium	Awareness campaigns, incentives
Regulatory challenges	Medium	Legal compliance frameworks

Step 7 — Implementation Timeline

Phase	Activities	Outcome
0–3 months	IT audit, planning, stakeholder alignment	Digital readiness baseline
3–6 months	Pilot e-governance & fin tech systems	Early adoption and testing
6–12 months	Expand marketplaces, integrate logistics	Revenue growth and efficiency
1–3 years	Full digital ecosystem scaling	Smart, integrated digital economy

Step 8 — Integration with Community & Economy

- Empower **SMEs, artisans, and local producers** through digital marketplaces
- Integrate digital platforms with **tourism, culture, and events economy**
- Use analytics to guide **city and state economic policy**
- Promote **Halal-compliant digital finance ecosystems**
- Strengthen **community participation** through digital engagement platforms

Conclusion

Technology and digital transformation are **multipliers of prosperity**. When implemented effectively, they:

- Increase **government efficiency and transparency**
- Generate **new revenue streams and economic activity**
- Empower citizens and local businesses
- Attract investment and innovation

By integrating **e-governance, fin tech, digital commerce, logistics, and data analytics**, neighborhoods, cities, and states can build a **resilient, inclusive, and globally competitive digital economy** that supports long-term prosperity and social cohesion.

Chapter 31 — Monitoring, Metrics, and Continuous Improvement

Objective

Sustainable prosperity is not static—it must be **continuously measured, evaluated, and refined.**

This chapter presents a structured framework for tracking **economic, social, and environmental performance** across neighborhoods, cities, and states. It enables **data-driven governance, accountability, and adaptive strategy execution**, ensuring that development remains effective, inclusive, and resilient.

Why Monitoring Matters

Performance Visibility

Monitor revenue generation, service delivery efficiency, and citizen engagement in real time.

Early Problem Detection

Identify inefficiencies, underperforming programs, and operational bottlenecks before they escalate.

Continuous Improvement

Refine policies and initiatives using evidence, analytics, and trend-based insights.

Transparency and Accountability

Strengthen trust among citizens, investors, and institutions through open reporting systems.

Evidence-Based Planning

Use reliable data to guide public policy, infrastructure investment, and social programs.

Case References

- **Smart Nation Singapore KPIs** – Integrated national dashboards monitoring sustainability, economic output, and citizen satisfaction

- **Dubai Monitoring Dashboards** – Real-time tracking of municipal services, tourism, and digital governance
- **Indonesia Village Scorecards** – Community-based evaluation tools driving rural development performance

Step 1 — Design the Monitoring & Evaluation (M&E) Framework

Key Performance Indicators (KPIs)

Economic Indicators

- Revenue growth and fiscal balance
- SME performance and entrepreneurship activity
- Investment inflows and job creation

Social Indicators

- Employment rates
- Literacy and education outcomes
- Healthcare access and coverage
- Citizen satisfaction and participation

Environmental Indicators

- Energy consumption and efficiency
- Carbon emissions and climate impact
- Green spaces and environmental quality

Data Collection & Sources

- Government databases and municipal systems
- IoT sensors and smart infrastructure
- Digital platforms (e-governance, fin tech, marketplaces)

- Community surveys and stakeholder feedback

Reporting Systems

- Real-time dashboards for neighborhoods, cities, and state authorities
- Periodic reports for investors, NGOs, and citizens
- Public transparency portals for open data access

Audits & Compliance

- Financial audits
- Project and operational reviews
- Environmental compliance assessments

Step 2 — Strategic Approach

Integrated M&E System

Develop a **multi-layered monitoring system** that connects neighborhood, city, and state-level data.

KPI Alignment

- Map indicators to economic, social, and environmental goals
- Include short-, medium-, and long-term metrics

Dashboard Development

- Visualize performance in real time
- Ensure access for policymakers, investors, and community leaders

Feedback Loops

- Community councils
- Mobile reporting apps

- Online citizen engagement platforms

Periodic Review

- Monthly operational reviews
- Quarterly performance evaluations
- Annual strategic updates

Cross-Scale Integration

- Ensure interoperability of data systems
- Consolidate local data into national policy insights

Step 3 — Monitoring & Continuous Improvement Checklist

Task	Description
KPI Identification	Define economic, social, and environmental indicators
Data Systems	Deploy IoT sensors, dashboards, and financial reporting tools
Reporting Channels	Enable dashboards, apps, and periodic reports
Audit Mechanisms	Conduct financial, operational, and environmental reviews
Feedback Systems	Use community forums, town halls, and digital platforms
Review Meetings	Schedule regular performance evaluations
Risk Monitoring	Identify data gaps, delays, and systemic biases

Step 4 — Integrated Monitoring & Evaluation Blueprint
Core Components

- **Data Sources:** Government, private sector, community, IoT systems

- **KPIs & Metrics:** Economic, social, environmental indicators
- **Dashboards & Visualization:** Real-time decision-making tools
- **Audits & Compliance:** Financial and operational oversight
- **Feedback Mechanisms:** Citizen and stakeholder engagement
- **Continuous Improvement:** Iterative planning and capacity building

System Structure

```
Integrated Monitoring & Evaluation (M&E) System
├── Data Collection
│   ├── Government
│   ├── Businesses
│   ├── Community
│   └── IoT/Technology
├── KPIs & Metrics
│   ├── Economic
│   ├── Social
│   └── Environmental
├── Dashboards & Reporting
├── Audits & Compliance Checks
├── Feedback Loops
└── Continuous Improvement & Strategy Updates
```

Step 5 — Business Model Canvas for Monitoring Systems

Block	Description
Value Proposition	Transparent, data-driven governance for sustainable prosperity
Key Activities	KPI tracking, reporting, audits, feedback management
Key Resources	Data analytics platforms, dashboards, IoT sensors, skilled staff
Key Partners	Technology firms, universities, NGOs, municipal agencies
Revenue Streams	Efficiency savings, performance-based funding, investor confidence
Cost Structure	IT systems, monitoring teams, audits, training
Customer Segments	Citizens, investors, planners, policymakers
Channels	Dashboards, mobile apps, websites, public meetings
Customer Relationships	Transparent, participatory, accountable
Metrics/KPIs	Revenue growth, citizen satisfaction, environmental compliance

Step 6 — Risk Assessment & Mitigation

Risk	Impact	Mitigation
Data integrity issues	High	Secure systems, audits, cross-verification
Delayed reporting	Medium	Automated dashboards and alerts
Misinterpretation of data	Medium	Training and expert advisory panels
Low engagement	Medium	Incentives, outreach, participatory platforms
KPI overdependence	Medium	Combine quantitative data with qualitative insights

Step 7 — Implementation Timeline

Phase	Activities	Outcome
Phase 1 (0–3 months)	KPI design, data audit, dashboard setup	M&E foundation established
Phase 2 (3–6 months)	Pilot dashboards, staff training, feedback systems	Early adoption and refinement
Phase 3 (6–12 months)	Full integration across regions	Real-time performance visibility
Phase 4 (1–3 years)	Continuous optimization and KPI updates	Adaptive, data-driven governance

Step 8 — Integration with Community & Prosperity Goals

- Align monitoring with economic growth, employment, healthcare, and education goals
- Use dashboards to identify service gaps and optimize resource allocation
- Encourage citizen participation in program evaluation
- Link performance outcomes to funding, PPPs, and investment decisions

Conclusion

An integrated Monitoring and Evaluation system ensures that prosperity initiatives remain **measurable, transparent, and continuously improving**.

By:

- Establishing comprehensive KPIs across economic, social, and environmental dimensions
- Implementing real-time dashboards and reporting systems
- Creating strong community feedback loops
- Conducting regular audits and applying insights

Neighborhoods, cities, and states can track progress, adapt strategies, and build a self-improving ecosystem of sustainable prosperity.

Chapter 32 — The 360° Prosperity Blueprint

Objective

This chapter synthesizes the entire framework into a **unified, multi-level prosperity system** that aligns national, state, city, and neighborhood initiatives into one coordinated ecosystem.

The aim is to create a **self-sustaining, resilient, and culturally aligned model of economic, social, and technological prosperity** for Muslim communities worldwide.

Why a 360° Blueprint Matters

Holistic Integration

Unifies fiscal systems, infrastructure, education, culture, technology, and entrepreneurship into one coherent strategy.

Efficiency & Synergy

Cross-level coordination eliminates duplication and maximizes resource utilization.

Scalable & Adaptable

Applicable from neighborhoods to nations, adaptable to different economic and cultural contexts.

Accountable & Measurable

Aligns KPIs, dashboards, and monitoring systems across all levels of governance.

Sustainability & Resilience

Ensures long-term economic, social, and environmental well-being.

Case References

- **Malaysia Shared Prosperity Vision 2030** — National

development aligned with state and local initiatives

- **Dubai Integrated Planning Model** — City projects coordinated with national economic diversification
- **Indonesia Village-to-National Funding System** — Grassroots development linked to national growth

Step 1 — Plan 360° Integration Across All Levels

National-Level Initiatives

- Trade, exports, energy, tourism, and fiscal policy
- Digital economy and national infrastructure
- Investment frameworks and diaspora engagement

State-Level Initiatives

- Industrial clusters and agriculture
- Healthcare systems and education networks
- Infrastructure and public-private partnerships

City-Level Initiatives

- Urban planning and smart city infrastructure
- Creative economy and tourism branding
- SME ecosystems and local marketplaces

Neighborhood-Level Initiatives

- Micro-entrepreneurship and cooperatives
- Halal markets and cultural festivals
- Workforce mapping and green spaces

Cross-Cutting Systems

- E-governance platforms
- Fin tech ecosystems
- Digital marketplaces
- KPI dashboards and M&E systems

Step 2 — Strategic Approach

Unified Prosperity Master plan

A coordinated governance model that connects **all layers of society and economy.**

Cross-Level Coordination

- Defined roles for national, state, city, and neighborhood authorities
- Regular coordination councils and digital collaboration systems

Stakeholder Alignment

- Citizens, businesses, NGOs, investors, and community leaders
- Transparent communication and shared ownership of development goals

Integrated Infrastructure Planning

- Synchronized transport, logistics, utilities, and digital networks
- Linking neighborhood initiatives to city and state hubs

Fiscal & Economic Integration

- Alignment of taxation, revenue collection, and investment flows
- Central financial dashboards tracking allocation and performance

Monitoring & Continuous Improvement

- Unified KPIs across all levels
- Real-time dashboards and performance analytics
- Data-driven policy optimization

Culture, Education & Technology Synergy

- Linking cultural industries with tourism and digital platforms
- Integrating education and workforce development into economic strategy

Step 3 — 360° Prosperity Blueprint Checklist

Task	Description
Cross-Level Coordination	Structured communication across all governance layers
Stakeholder Mapping	Identify partners, investors, NGOs, and community leaders
Resource Alignment	Optimize funding, land, infrastructure, and human capital
KPI Standardization	Unified economic, social, and environmental indicators
Feedback Systems	Citizen and business participation channels
Risk Assessment	Identify systemic and interdependent risks
Implementation Roadmap	Timelines, responsibilities, and review cycles

Step 4 — Unified Prosperity Master plan Blueprint

Core Components

- **Integrated Governance** — Cross-level councils and policy coordination
- **Financial & Investment Framework** — Multi-source funding and revenue systems
- **Infrastructure & Urban Systems** — Transport, energy, logistics, utilities
- **Economic Hubs** — SMEs, industry clusters, tourism, marketplaces
- **Cultural & Educational Ecosystem** — Schools, festivals, vocational training, Halal industries

- **Digital Transformation** — E-governance, fin tech, smart services
- **Monitoring & Evaluation** — KPIs, dashboards, audits, feedback loops
- **Sustainability Systems** — Renewable energy, green infrastructure, environmental protection

System Architecture

```
360° Prosperity Blueprint
 ├─ National Initiatives
 │   ├─ Trade & Exports
 │   ├─ Energy & Infrastructure
 │   └─ Investment & Diaspora Engagement
 ├─ State Initiatives
 │   ├─ Industrial Clusters
 │   ├─ Agriculture & Healthcare
 │   └─ Education & Skill Development
 ├─ City Initiatives
 │   ├─ Urban Planning & Smart City
 │   ├─ Creative Economy & Marketplaces
 │   └─ Civic Branding
 ├─ Neighborhood Initiatives
 │   ├─ Micro-Entrepreneurship
 │   ├─ Cultural Festivals & Green Spaces
 │   └─ Workforce & Skill Mapping
 └─ Cross-Cutting Systems
 ├─ Digital Platforms & IT Infrastructure
 ├─ Monitoring & KPI Dashboards
 └─ Continuous Improvement Systems
```

Step 5 — Full-Scale Business Model Canvas

Block	Description
Value Proposition	Sustainable, culturally aligned, self-sufficient prosperity ecosystem
Key Activities	Fiscal policy, infrastructure, SME development, culture, technology, M&E
Key Resources	Land, human capital, financial capital, technology, cultural assets
Key Partners	Government agencies, investors, NGOs, diaspora, technology providers
Revenue Streams	Taxes, exports, PPPs, tourism, digital services, local commerce
Cost Structure	Infrastructure, education, health, governance, technology systems
Customer Segments	Citizens, businesses, investors, tourists, diaspora communities
Channels	Digital platforms, physical infrastructure, community networks
Customer Relationships	Participatory, transparent, accountable, feedback-driven
Metrics/KPIs	Revenue growth, employment, education, sustainability, digital adoption

Step 6 — Risk Assessment & Mitigation

Risk	Impact	Mitigation
Misalignment across levels	High	Cross-level councils, digital coordination
Funding gaps	Medium	Multi-source funding and PPP strategies
Data gaps	Medium	Integrated M&E dashboards and analytics
Stakeholder resistance	Medium	Engagement campaigns and incentives
Environmental & social risks	High	Sustainability KPIs and impact assessments

Step 7 — Implementation Timeline

Phase	Activities	Outcome
Phase 1 (0–6 months)	Planning, stakeholder mapping, resource assessment	Baseline framework established
Phase 2 (6–12 months)	Pilot integration in selected areas	Proof of concept and KPI validation
Phase 3 (12–24 months)	Expand to city-state integration, launch digital systems	Measurable progress and optimization
Phase 4 (24–60 months)	National-scale rollout and continuous improvement	Fully operational prosperity ecosystem

Step 8 — Integration, Legacy, and Global Impact

Unified Vision

Prosperity is a shared, multi-level responsibility—no community is left behind.

Cultural & Economic Balance

Economic growth aligns with heritage, faith, and social cohesion.

Sustainability & Resilience

Infrastructure, governance, and economy are designed for long-term stability.

Replication & Global Scaling

The framework can be adapted to Muslim communities worldwide.

Accountable Legacy

Transparent monitoring ensures every initiative delivers measurable benefits to citizens.

Conclusion

The **360° Prosperity Blueprint** transforms fragmented development efforts into a **single, cohesive, and scalable system** that ensures:

- Economic self-sufficiency and growth
- Social equity and inclusive development
- Cultural preservation and creative industry expansion
- Technological advancement and digital transformation
- Continuous monitoring, learning, and improvement

When implemented effectively, this blueprint enables Muslim neighborhoods, cities, states, and nations to emerge as self-reliant, prosperous, and globally competitive communities—leaving a legacy of dignity, resilience, and innovation for future generations.

Conclusion

Revenue, Growth, and Development for Muslim Communities" is not just a manual—it is a comprehensive roadmap for economic, social, and cultural flourishing. Across neighborhoods, cities, states, and nations, the book offers practical strategies, actionable checklists, blueprints, and business canvases designed to empower communities to:

- Achieve economic self-sufficiency through diversified revenue streams, trade, investment, and innovation.
- Strengthen governance and civic institutions, ensuring transparency, accountability, and strategic planning at every level.
- Leverage culture, education, and technology as engines of development, creating wealth while preserving heritage.
- Build resilient neighborhoods and thriving cities, where citizens actively participate in shaping their own prosperity.
- Implement a 360° integrated system, aligning national, state, city, and neighborhood initiatives into a unified, measurable framework.

This book emphasizes that prosperity is **holistic, participatory, and data-driven**. By combining fiscal insight, urban planning, technological innovation, cultural preservation, and community engagement, it offers a **replicable model** for Muslim communities worldwide to grow sustainably, responsibly, and with dignity.

Ultimately, the book leaves readers with both **a vision and a toolkit**—a framework that transforms aspiration into action, and ambition into measurable, lasting impact.

About the Author

Fazal Abubakkar Esaf is a visionary author, strategist, and thought leader in community development, economic planning, and cultural prosperity. With extensive experience in policy advisory, entrepreneurship ecosystems, and socio-economic research, he has dedicated his work to creating practical frameworks for sustainable growth within Muslim communities worldwide.

Esaf combines **deep analytical insight** with **actionable strategies**, effectively bridging the gap between high-level planning and grassroots implementation. His work is defined by a strong commitment to **cultural authenticity, innovation, and participatory governance**, aiming to empower communities to thrive economically, soçially, and culturally.

Through his research, workshops, and publications, **Fazal Abubakkar Esaf** inspires leaders, policymakers, and citizens alike to **think systemically, act decisively, and build prosperity that endures for generations.**

Don't miss out!

Visit the website below and you can sign up to receive emails whenever Fazal Abubakkar Esaf publishes a new book. There's no charge and no obligation.

https://books2read.com/r/B-A-KTQWD-UFDBJ

BOOKS 2 READ

Connecting independent readers to independent writers.

Did you love *Revenue, Growth, and Development for Muslim Communities*? Then you should read *Rebuilding Muslim Economies*[1] by Fazal Abubakkar Esaf!

[2]

Why Muslim Economies Need a New Development Conversation

Across regions as diverse as South Asia, the Middle East, North Africa, and parts of Sub-Saharan Africa, Muslim-majority countries present a striking paradox. Many possess abundant natural resources, strategic geography, large and youthful populations, and deep historical trading networks—yet struggle to translate these advantages into broad-based prosperity.

The explanation most often offered is identity-based, rooted in culture, religion, or historical grievance. This book rejects that narrative.

---

1. https://books2read.com/u/bplo5q

2. https://books2read.com/u/bplo5q

The real constraints are institutional.

Weak rule of law, elite capture of economic rents, the exclusion of women and youth, under- performing education systems, fragmented markets, and politicized bureaucracies have collectively produced growth that is either unsustainable or deeply unequal. Where growth has occurred, it has often failed to generate employment, resilience, or social trust.

This book argues that economic reform must begin with governance reform, followed by market restructuring, sustained investment in human capital, and ethical—but not ideological—economic frameworks.

Also by Fazal Abubakkar Esaf

Silent Streets
The Wind doesn't keep Diaries
Stress Free Teachers
Pardon My Cabinet
The Muslim Room You never Visited
Three Bullets,Two Bodies,One Lie
I Met You between Heartbeats
Chronicles from the Forbidden Future
The Garden within the House
The Garden within the House
The Silence Beneath the Soul
Meadow Days & Candlelight Nights
When Love withers in Silence
And Still, We Loved Again
Everyday Battles: Fight, Faith, Future
Love that lives in wounds
Monsoon Inside Room
Pure Joy Bonds
Nowhere to Belong
Voices in the Riddim
Loving You Was a War I Lost Beautifully
Map of You in Me
The Echo Within the Silence
Wolves Eat the Wind
Love Stories in the Language of Rain and Ruins

Nafs Unveiled: A Journey into the Healing Heart of the Soul
The Banana Leaf Was Still Warm
The Pandemic Diaries
Love in the Long Queue
Maps Left in Rain
Rumours from the Coconut Wireless
The Streets Between Us
Where the Sky Drinks the Sea
The Beautiful Lie We Live
Fingerprint of Crimes
Tides of Silence, Shores of Renewal
We Were a Poem with No Ending
He Loved Me in Parentheses
Whispers Between Walls
Khaki Reflection: voices from the uniform
Glass Shadows: Poems
River Without Source
Another Night with No Cigarettes
The Road North and Other Stories
Whispers Between Memory and the City
Reflections on Meaning and Suffering
The Psychology of Collective Tales
Footprints in the Monsoon Mist
The Inner Road of the Waking Man
Whispers and Wings
Between Concrete and Dust
India's Riots A People's Guide to History, Causes, and Healing.
Politics without Illusions
Lives Between Thought and Silence
Ordinary Dust, Living Stories
Stories of Memory, Identity, and Urban Lives
Rebuilding Muslim Economies
When the Azan Meets the Morning Sun

Where The City Leaves its Shadows
After the War: What Remains
Beyond Division: Psychology, Strategy, and the Politics of Harmony
The Refugee Experience
Muslims in Contemporary India
The Unsaid Lives of Enclosed Spaces
From Death to Truth
Narrative Residue
Whispers of the Courtyard
Echoes of the Human Soul
Quiet Truths
Ten Percent Human
Silent Pursuit
The Reflective Waters of the Heart
When No One Is Left
Maratha's Complete Art of Asymmetric War
Political Strategy Lessons from Maratha Commanders
Evidence Doesn't Always Cast Shadows
Invisible To Accountable
Lives of Incomplete People
The Last Question
Ghosts Were Never the Killers
Suspect by Default
Unopposed
Lives Misread
When Machines Learn To Feel
When Time Walked Slower
Between Clocks and Snow
Saffron Light and Other Stories
Silence, Memory, and the Human Heart
Journey Smart
The Night of a Thousand Lanterns
All The Ways We Laugh

Lives between the Bills
Gandhi's Way Today
Anatomy of a Broken Place
The Ordinary Man Who Outran the World
White Coats, Dark Wounds
City Of Shadows
The Architecture of Corruption
When the Maps Forget Us
Death as a Counselor
In Search of the Nameless Truth
The Anatomy of a Con
The Architecture of Power
The Wind That Refuses Obedience
Ultimate Personal Security Blueprint
Prisoners of Their Own Neurons
The Invisible Empire
When the Mind Breaks Quietly
Faithwealth
Revenue, Growth, and Development for Muslim Communities
BioShield Protocol
Muslims under the Gaze of Empire

www.ingramcontent.com/pod-product-compliance
Lightning Source LLC
LaVergne TN
LVHW090320210926
848480LV00001B/309